Project Cost Management

Project Cost Management
Principles, Tools, Techniques, and Best Practices for Project Finance

Second Edition

Ray W. Frohnhoefer and Inham Hassen

Project Cost Management: Principles, Tools, Techniques, and Best Practices for Project Finance, Second Edition

© Copyright 2026 Ray W. Frohnhoefer and Inham Hassen

All Rights Reserved. No part of this book may be reproduced, stored, or transmitted in any form or by any means, including electronic, mechanical, photocopying, recording, or otherwise, without the written prior permission from the publisher, except in the case of brief quotations embodied in critical articles and reviews. Please purchase only legitimate copies and support authors' rights.

The author and publisher have attempted to verify copyright holders of all material and apologize if permission to publish in this form has not been given. If any copyrighted material has not been acknowledged, please contact us to make corrections.

ISBN-13: 978-1-7356213-3-3 (paperback)
ISBN-13: 978-1-7356213-4-0 (e-book)

Cover design by Jonas Peres
Copyediting aided by Microsoft Word and Grammarly
References supported by Zotero
Indexing supported by Indexia

For information about copyright, permissions, bulk discounts, or purchase, contact:

PPC Group, LLC
3450 3rd Avenue
Suite 309
San Diego, CA 92103
USA
https://ppcgroup.us
https://accidentalpm.online
http://rayfrohnhoefer.com

"PMI," "PMBOK," and the PMI logo are service marks and trademarks of the Project Management Institute, Inc., regulated in the USA and other nations. Microsoft, Excel, PowerPoint, Word, Outlook, and Windows are registered trademarks or trademarks of the Microsoft group of companies. This book's other product and company names may be trademarks or registered trademarks of their respective owners. Except for the authors and publisher, no companies participated in the development of this book or have any financial interest in its publication.

About the Author – Ray Frohnhoefer

Ray Frohnhoefer is the Managing Partner of PPC Group, LLC, helping aspiring, new, and accidental project managers and their organizations improve project management practice. Products and services include international bestsellers in Business Project Management, education, corporate training, and consulting.

Ray has led consulting teams in many industries and locations over his 40-year career. Notable projects include:

- rolling out a UNIX development environment to 400+ developers in 16 locations
- testing electronic voting equipment with a team of 30 for San Diego County
- patenting an estimating tool used by a global Project Management Office.

No stranger to virtual and global teams, he has worked with them throughout his career.

Ray has had a dual career in project management and training. For eight years, he was an author, editor, and lecturer for the Edison Engineering Advanced Course in Computers. In addition, he has taught project management and business analysis courses for UC San Diego's Division of Extended Studies for 18 years.

A long-time Project Management Institute (PMI) volunteer, Ray served as President of the PMI San Diego Chapter in 2005. In 2006, he was the first official PMI Region Mentor for Southwest North America. In addition, he has supported several international PMI committees and groups over the past 15 years. Ray also helped the PMI Educational Foundation establish its first professional development scholarship.

Ray holds an undergraduate degree in Mathematics with a concentration in Computer Science and an MBA in Technology Management. He is a graduate of the PMI Leadership Institute Master Class (LIMC) and a Certified Computer Professional (CCP).

About the Author – M. Inham Hassen

Inham Hassen became a project manager by accident. Since beginning his project management journey, he has delivered projects in the UK, Europe, South Asia, the Far East, and Africa. These projects include telecommunications network rollouts, large-scale post-merger integrations, core banking system implementations, COVID-19 emergency response programs, and digital transformations.

He holds a master's degree in IT Management from Carnegie Mellon University, an LLM in Law from the University of Sunderland, and an Electrical Engineering degree from the Indian Institute of Technology. Furthermore, he possesses PMP, PRINCE2 Practitioner, MoP Practitioner, P3O Practitioner, and PMO Value Ring Certified Practitioner certifications. In addition, he is an accredited trainer in PRINCE2 and MoP.

He actively works with the global project management community to enhance the profession. He is a member of the judging committee for the annual award for the world's best-run project management office (organized by the PMO Global Alliance). Inham is a reviewer for P3.express, a European Commission-funded minimalistic project management methodology, and the author of an MoP Foundation study guide. He created the world's first MoP Foundation exam simulator and the world's first and only Wiki for Project Portfolio Management (MoP.wiki).

He was awarded the Fellowship of the Royal Society of Arts in the UK in 2021.

Dedication

I dedicate this book to my husband, who always supports my work.

Moreover, for my readers and fellow project managers, it is crucial to strengthen your skills in a rapidly evolving workplace. Never stop learning.

—Ray

I dedicate this book to

• My teachers at Wesley College, Colombo, Sri Lanka, who are the reason for where I am now.

• My wife, for her love, care, and extraordinary ability to tolerate me.

—Inham

Table of Contents

INTRODUCTION TO PROJECT COST MANAGEMENT (AND THE FINANCE PERFORMANCE DOMAIN) 1

PART I: COST MANAGEMENT PROCESSES AND PRINCIPLES 5

CHAPTER 1: FINANCIAL PERFORMANCE DOMAIN PROCESSES 7

CHAPTER 2: THE TIME VALUE OF MONEY 19

CHAPTER 3: PRINCIPLES AND BEST PRACTICES FOR SUCCESS 27

PART II: CREATING AND FUNDING THE BUDGET (INITIATION THROUGH PLANNING) 35

CHAPTER 4: PROJECT SELECTION TECHNIQUES USING COST 37

CHAPTER 5: FINANCE PERFORMANCE PLANNING 53

CHAPTER 6: COST ESTIMATION TECHNIQUES 61

CHAPTER 7: THE BASICS OF BUDGETS 81

CHAPTER 8: BUDGET PRESENTATION 95

CHAPTER 9: PROJECT FINANCING 103

CHAPTER 10: PROJECT PAYMENTS 117

PART III: MONITORING AND CONTROLLING COSTS (FROM EXECUTION THROUGH CLOSEOUT) 123

CHAPTER 11: TOOLS AND TECHNIQUES FOR COST CONTROL 125

CHAPTER 12: AN INTRODUCTION TO EARNED VALUE MANAGEMENT 139

CHAPTER 13: CONTRACTS AND WORK AUTHORIZATION SYSTEMS 153

CHAPTER 14: PROJECT CASH FLOW MANAGEMENT 165

CHAPTER 15: COST MANAGEMENT AND PROJECT CLOSEOUT 171

CHAPTER 16: ARTIFICIAL INTELLIGENCE TOOLS 181

REFERENCES **189**

APPENDIX A: LICENSE TO USE AND MODIFY TEMPLATES AND INSTRUCTIONAL MATERIALS **193**

APPENDIX B: RULES OF ROUNDING **195**

APPENDIX C: MORE ABOUT PERT **199**

INDEX **205**

List of Figures, Tables, and Equations

Figure 1: An Estimation Framework 71
Figure 2: Sample WBS-based Budget 98
Figure 3: Sample Activity-based Budget 99
Figure 4: Sample Time-Phased Budget with Alternative Format 100
Figure 5: Four Basic Corrective Actions 127
Figure 6: Budget Control Chart Example 130
Figure 7: Project J-curve vs. S-curve 131
Figure 8: EVMS Status Reporting Format 151
Figure 9: Sample Cash Flow 167
Figure 10: PERT Example 200
Figure 11: Completed PERT Example 200
Figure 12: Applying the Normal Distribution Curve to Potential Budgets... 202
Figure 13: Applying the Normal Distribution Curve Inverse Function to Potential Probabilities 203

Table 1: Contributions to Budget by PMBOK Performance Domain 15
Table 2: Sample Depreciation 87
Table 3: Essential Earned Value Management Terms' 140
Table 4: Additional Earned Value Management Terms for Forecasting....... 145
Table 5: Contract Type Comparison 159

Equation 1: Future Value 21
Equation 2: Present Value 22
Equation 3: Return on Assets 43
Equation 4: Return on Average Capital Employed 43
Equation 5: Return on Investment 43
Equation 6: Net Present Value 44
Equation 7: Payback Period 45
Equation 8: Triangular Distribution or 3-Point Estimate 64
Equation 9: PERT Estimation with 95% Confidence 66
Equation 10: Straight-line Depreciation 88
Equation 11: Contingency Reserve Calculation 90
Equation 12: Calculating the Cost of Capital 112
Equation 13: Cost and Schedule Variance 143
Equation 14: Cost and Schedule Performance Indices 144
Equation 15: Estimate at Completion 146
Equation 16: Estimate to Complete and Variance at Completion 146
Equation 17: To Complete Performance Index 147
Equation 18: Excel Normal Distribution Function 202
Equation 19: Excel NORMINV Function 202

Preface

As with my previous books, this book draws on my career-long work and learning. My interest in cost management and finance began in the late 70s, when a proposed project was rejected. Management explained that the company would not invest in a product provided to clients at no charge. I consulted with our Finance Department and found that, without this free product, nearly two-thirds of the company's revenue would evaporate. I learned this was known as "pull-through revenue." The project was approved with this discovery.

This incident sparked my interest, and I enrolled in a program to train as a company auditor while continuing to manage projects. Unfortunately, it was not for the position; many of the clients I supported on software projects were financial institutions. Ironic, given that I had no budget responsibility this early in my project management career. I worked exclusively with human resources, so management's interest was in time. The Finance Department managed most of the actual budgets.

In 1990, due to a senior management error, I had the opportunity to set and manage a modest project budget. This work and subsequent experience enabled me to manage projects for insurance companies, the integration and implementation of PeopleSoft Financials, and other financial software projects throughout the 90s. I completed an MBA in 2000 with a minor in Finance.

From 2003 until 2020, I taught a course for UC San Diego's Division of Extended Studies titled Controlling Project Costs and Risks. Cost management accounted for approximately one-third of the material, with a primary focus on creating and managing project budgets. It underwent approximately four revisions during that period and was subsequently split into two classes: Project Cost Management and Project Risk Management. This doubled the content in each area.

When the class was split, I had just finished *Risk Assessment Framework: Successfully Navigating Uncertainty*. However, I found no coverage of cost management, so I sought alternatives. I found books dedicated to specific industries (especially construction) or to specific aspects of cost management. For example:

- Cost control
- Cost from an accounting viewpoint
- Cost from the Association for the Advancement of Cost Engineering viewpoint

Unfortunately, there has been only one book in the last ten to twenty years that is "comprehensive" on project cost management. Still, it is very short and largely echoes the PMBOK Guide, offering little in the way of "how-to" information.

After reviewing these sources, I developed an expanded course outline. I added material on cost and project initiation, cash flow management (critical for many construction projects), and expanded on existing cost control material.

My goal has always been to address critical knowledge areas beyond those covered in the Accidental Project Management books. In 2021, I began expanding my course outline into a full-length text. That year, I also partnered with Inham Hassen to develop this book. Inham has strong management and editing skills and brings a PMO and international perspective to the book. I am honored to work with him to complete this book.

This book aims to be clear enough for accidental, new, or aspiring project managers to understand, yet sufficiently comprehensive for experienced project managers (similar to the *Risk Assessment Framework*). We believe we broadly cover all aspects of cost management and address gaps left by spotty coverage, given the few new and significant books in the field. As with other PPC Group books, tips, and templates, support the text.

I hope you enjoy this book as much as we have enjoyed working on it!

- Ray W. Frohnhoefer
San Diego, California, USA
May 2022

New in the Second Edition

The main purpose of the second edition is to align the contents to the PMBOK Guide, Eighth Edition. The Cost Management knowledge area is now referred to as the Finance Performance Domain, and the process groups are now called "Focus Areas." We've retained the title, *Project Cost Management*, to identify the book, since the new Finance performance domain still focuses on costs.

The second edition presented an opportunity to make numerous improvements, including:

- Terminology and minor changes to align with the PMBOK Guide, Eighth Edition
- Added to the project selection cost metrics of Chapter 4
- Reworked Chapter 6 on estimation, expanding information regarding agile and hybrid methods and artificial intelligence support
- Reworked Chapter 13 on contracts, adding work authorization systems
- Added Chapter 16 on Artificial Intelligence Tools
- Updated and improved all chapter summaries
- Numerous editorial, copyedit, and layout improvements to both print and ebooks
- Updated Table of Contents, References, and Index

Acknowledgments

So many people are involved in this book that the best way to begin is: “We are sorry if we have left out your name.”

First, we would like to thank Dr. John Estrella. John is an incredible business coach and mentor – all of us who work with him have experienced extraordinary transformations in our businesses. Without John's guidance, this book would probably still be an idea.

Next, we would like to thank the many global professionals who have helped by reading, editing, or giving feedback and guidance for this book: Chuck Adams (USA), Shaham Anam (Sweden), Shweta Brahmakshatriya (India), Naomi Caietti (USA), John Estrella (Canada), Sumith Kahanda (Canada), Nitin Kundeshwar (USA), Deasún Ó Conchúir (Switzerland), Renjith Suresh Padma (India), Harjit Singh (USA), Peeyush Thakur (Canada), Kashif Zafeer (Kuwait).

Finally, we thank our colleagues and students for the information and feedback over time that have shaped this book.

#PROJECTCOSTMANAGEMENT

Introduction To Project Cost Management (And the Finance Performance Domain)

The cost management knowledge area of project management focuses on planning, estimating, budgeting, and controlling expenditures to ensure they remain within the project's approved budget. The PMBOK Guide, Eighth Edition, now refers to this knowledge as the Finance Performance Domain. Overall, the language has shifted from “process groups” to “areas of focus” and from “knowledge areas” to “performance domains.”

While the processes in the finance performance domain largely mirror those in the cost knowledge area, the PMBOK Guide places greater emphasis on delivering value and benefits and on sustainability. It may sound simple, but identifying all project costs is perhaps the most challenging task for a project manager and team. In addition to basic resource costs, additional charges may arise from economic conditions, equipment operating expenses, loan and bond repayments, and other expenses.

To effectively estimate, document, and manage costs, project managers must navigate national, state, local, and, at times, international and corporate financial regulations and organizational practices. Therefore, practitioners require the greatest flexibility in this area and must collaborate with management and financial professionals to determine the precise scope of their financial roles and responsibilities.

No organization has unlimited financial resources; therefore, project cost management is relevant to all projects, regardless of the management methods employed. Predictive[1] (aka Waterfall) projects have the most detail available for budgeting. The project schedule and resources inform the costs of each activity or task. Summing these costs yields the budget; this is a bottom-up approach.

Agile project management methods rely on less accurate estimates and are generally less focused on cost. The initial budget is often top-down, based on experience and judgment. Steps may be required to translate story-point estimates into monetary values. Backlog items with higher story points may require further breakdown to determine costs—the details of charges are only known at the end of each sprint.

Therefore, the project management practitioner must account for cost goals when selecting projects. For example, projects with fixed funding or those requiring more robust cost control may benefit from predictive or hybrid methods (e.g., a combination of

---

[1] If you do not understand fundamental project management terminology, we highly recommend that you read *Accidental Project Manager: Zero to Hero in 7 Days* and/or *Accidental Agile Project Manager: Zero to Hero in 7 Iterations* first. This book builds on the basic project management knowledge presented in these books. Another valuable resource is the *PMI Lexicon of Project Management Terms*.

predictive, iterative, and agile approaches) to achieve optimal outcomes. Combining these methods is also significant, as predictive methods offer the best opportunities for cost control.

This book provides a comprehensive guide to project cost management for readers with a fundamental understanding of project management. Rather than focusing solely on the budget, this book covers financial concepts for project selection, estimation, payments, financing, and control throughout the project lifecycle. We have made every effort to keep concepts clear for aspiring, new, and accidental project managers while covering project financial topics relevant to all project managers.

PART I: COST MANAGEMENT PROCESSES AND PRINCIPLES

"Remember that time is money. He that can earn ten shillings a day by his labour, and goes abroad, or sits idle one half of that day, though he spends but sixpence during his diversion or idleness, it ought not to be reckoned the only expence; he hath really spent or thrown away five shillings besides."

– Benjamin Franklin

CHAPTER 1

Chapter 1: Financial Performance Domain Processes

The financial performance domain (formerly the cost management knowledge area) processes in the PMBOK® Guide are deceptively simple. They aim to create a budget and monitor progress against it. Unfortunately, real-world projects are not always as simple as the project manager may hope.

Many planning processes impact cost management. For example, estimating costs can be challenging without knowing resource needs over time. Additionally, the project manager may need to work with a procurement specialist to purchase materials and develop contracts. Further, large, complex, and mega-projects will have financing and payment terms that are difficult to estimate and track.

It is also helpful for the project manager to understand the basics of portfolio and program cost management. The understanding will provide insight into management thinking and preferences that will be important for later decision-making. The first section of this book and the chapter, "Project Selection Techniques Using Cost," will help set the stage for cost management at the project level.

Before getting into the "nuts and bolts" of financial performance, let us briefly look at each standard process.

Plan Financial Management

The Plan Financial Management (formerly Plan Cost Management) process uses known project information from the project charter, project management plan, other project documents, and conditions to specify how project revenues[2] and costs will be managed and controlled. The PMBOK® Guide outlines the "how" but does not provide sufficient detail to enable you to complete an effective plan.

A reasonable financial management plan is largely reusable. Therefore, having a good one is essential. The chapter "Finance Management Planning" reviews the critical and optional components. Further, please see Appendix A for access to the financial management plan template.

Estimate Costs

The Estimate Costs process estimates the project's cost and resource requirements. The most effective approach is to use the Work Breakdown Structure (WBS); however, other methods are also available.

---

[2] Project revenues were added in the PMBOK Guide, Eighth Edition. Although not included in budgets, project revenue forecasts are now part of the Monitor and Control Finance process.

The project manager must revisit estimates and the budget throughout the project. The cost represented in the project charter is usually an executive "guess" or the amount the organization has budgeted for the project. It is not easy to achieve accuracy without knowing exactly how the work will be done. Therefore, as project planning progresses, the estimates should be revisited.

When the WBS is complete, it is an opportunity. Once the work packages are known, compare their estimates to the initiation estimate. Some long-term projects should be reestimated once more details are available, such as when requirements or the project design are complete. A re-estimate will ensure accuracy and avoid unexpected costs later.

The chapter "Cost Estimation Techniques" will thoroughly cover cost estimation and includes a template for applying the PERT method. PERT is a powerful tool for accurate estimates and answering "what if" questions about the forecast costs. While designed initially for schedule estimates, it is equally applicable to costs.

Determine Budget

Determine Budget aggregates costs by category and unit for financial reporting. The organization or its finance department often sets these categories. The project cost baseline should represent all funds needed to complete the project. At this point, the budget may or may not include contingency reserves, based on local practice. The need for contingency reserves requires an understanding of project risks, as they are intended to cover them.

While not part of the cost baseline, management reserves are also needed to account for risks that may arise but have not yet been identified. This amount becomes the total project budget when added to the cost baseline.

The project requires funds to be available once the budget has been created and approved. Budgets are funded by organizations that specify how often budget increments should be made available. For example, the frequency could be from "all at once" to "on-demand" to monthly, quarterly, or annually. The funding requirements may also specify the sources and other attributes of funds.

For example, a project manager we know managed projects to develop and install customized software packages for schools, and many school financial years run from July of one year to June of the following year. This timeline requires all projects to have estimates submitted by June. In June, the school sets aside or encumbers these funds. As projects progressed, the project manager would ensure monthly billing.

Running over budget was a huge problem. If this happens, the school administrators must meet to decide on the new amount. However, these meetings are infrequent, and allocating additional funds throughout the year may not be feasible. So it was critical to have reasonable estimates and budgets up front.

This book provides essential knowledge to help project managers avoid similar issues. Multiple chapters cover budgets and items that impact them:

- The Basics of Budgets covers terminology and fundamental concepts related to budgets
- Budget Presentation covers how to document and present a budget

- Project Financing and Project Payments explores financing terms and invoicing payments; they are planning considerations

Monitor and Control Finances

Monitor and Control Finances is the process by which project managers monitor progress against the cost baseline and budget. The project manager needs to ensure sound monitoring. Simply subtracting billed dollars from the budget is unlikely to be sufficient for many projects. One notable San Diego project, the construction of Petco Park, found that this approach made it easy to spend 100% of the budget even when only half the work was done. Some sophistication and finesse are required to avoid issues.

The last section of this book is devoted to project cost management during execution, monitoring and control, and project closure.

Financial Performance and Other Domains

Financial performance domain processes directly impact the Governance, Scope, and Schedule performance domains and may, directly or indirectly, affect other performance domains. Fundamentally, time is money, and these areas contribute to project costs. It is easiest to see this when looking at the project management knowledge areas.

Scope Performance Domain. Determining the proper scope guides team decision-making about the work to be performed. Knowing what work to complete guides the estimation process. The output estimates will form the basis for the budget.

Project changes will also add to costs. Therefore, change requests must include an investigation of the financial impact. Once changes are agreed upon, their costs must not be charged to contingency reserves; they must be added separately to the budget and tracked.

Just as time is money, quality comes at a cost. As demand for quality rises, costs rise as well. It is not uncommon for project managers of knowledge-based projects (e.g., software development, technology) to neglect adding time and costs for testing resources and project closeout. As a result, these projects often reach 95% completion and remain there, consuming physical and financial resources. To avoid getting stuck, exit criteria must be clear, and compromises may be necessary to protect financial resources.

Schedule Performance Domain. The schedule is a roadmap for project completion, showing who does what and when. Resource cost information includes the periods the resources are used, which are factored into the budget.

Project changes will also change when resources are needed. It is crucial to consider new costs and costs that may change in response to a change request.

Governance Performance Domain. Governance policies and decisions, such as the project delivery method (e.g., Predictive, Agile, or Hybrid), affect the budget and its monitoring. For example, predictive projects usually have comprehensive, detailed budgets subject to strict change control, while agile and hybrid budgets may be less strict and more flexible.

Project governance spans all project focus areas. Project initiation provides a project charter. The charter includes high-level information about the work and expected costs.

With the project charter as input, planning begins, and the Work Breakdown Structure may provide the initial cost estimates. As planning progresses, a budget is formed. During execution, monitor work progress and changes, and ensure you understand performance against scope, schedule, and cost.

Project closeout is a critical time and focus area in which many project managers underestimate expenses. Development of training, documentation, acceptance test cases, health and safety requirements, and regulatory requirements all add to costs. Some of these costs may need to be carried over into operations budgets. Moreover, it is critical to provide excellent support as projects transition to operations.

Resource Performance Domain. A thorough identification of project resources is necessary to develop the best schedule and, by extension, budget. In addition to acquiring resources, their operation may incur costs. For example, some operations may require sustained support over time (e.g., construction equipment paid for on an hourly basis that requires fuel). Therefore, another cost component is the period for which resources are needed.

Project changes also alter resource requirements, increasing the cost of change requests.

Stakeholder Performance Domain. The generation and distribution of project communications to stakeholders adds to project costs. Therefore, it is critical to add these to the project budget. Project communications also need to meet stakeholders' information needs regarding project financial performance.

Risk Performance Domain. Risks have positive and negative financial impacts on projects. These impacts play a critical role in determining project contingency reserves.

It is also crucial to consider that risk management activities consume resources and incur associated costs. Therefore, include these activities and resources in project schedules and budgets.

Project Procurement Management. Procurement encompasses all aspects of a company's purchasing of goods and services. Large projects often require dedicated procurement specialists to ensure the required goods and services are in place as the project progresses. Considering procurement requirements and timelines early in a project helps plan and manage finances more effectively.

One crucial planning aspect is the timing of overseas shipments. Depending on the countries of origin and destination, import taxes, tariffs, and duties may increase costs.

Governance	Establishes spending authority, approval thresholds, and controls (e.g., baselines, change control, stage gates) that determine how funds are authorized and released.
Scope	Defines what is included or excluded and the required quality level, which drives estimating, procurement, and the size of contingency for scope change and rework.
Schedule	Impacts budget through time-dependent costs (labor, facilities, rentals), schedule compression premiums, and the cost effects of delays or idle time.
Finance	Produces the budget and cost baseline, identifies funding sources and timing, and ties spending to value measures (e.g., ROI/NPV) and financial constraints.
Stakeholders	Shapes budget for communications, engagement activities, and expectation management; reduces the likelihood of costly late changes, disputes, or acceptance delays.
Resources	Drives the cost of staffing, skills, training, productivity, tools, and sourcing choices (in-house vs. vendor), including ramp-up/ramp-down and turnover costs.
Risk	Translates uncertainties into budget reserves, informs cost of risk responses, and prevents cost overruns from realized threats.

Table 1: Contributions to Budget by PMBOK Performance Domain

Chapter Summary

Chapter 1 introduces the financial performance domain and explains how project budgets are created, refined, and monitored throughout the project lifecycle. Although the PMBOK Guide's processes appear straightforward—*"create a budget and monitor progress against it"*—real projects involve complexities such as procurement timing, resource availability, and organizational funding cycles.

The chapter reviews the four core processes:

- **Plan Financial Management**, which defines how costs and revenues will be managed;
- **Estimate Costs**, which relies on the WBS and requires revisiting early "executive guesses" as planning matures;
- **Determine Budget**, which aggregates estimates into a cost baseline and incorporates contingency and management reserves; and
- **Monitor and Control Finances**, which requires more than simply subtracting spending from the budget, since this can mask true progress.

Finally, the chapter shows how financial performance interacts with all other performance domains. Scope, schedule, governance, resources, stakeholders, risk, and procurement each influence project costs and must be considered when planning and managing the budget. *"Time is money,"* and effective financial management depends on understanding these interdependencies.

Knowledge Nuggets

Chapter Pro Tip: The financial performance domain requires greater flexibility than other project management knowledge areas to align with organizational norms.

In many organizations, financial standards and practices are more influenced by existing norms than by other project management knowledge areas. These circumstances, often created to support the Finance Department and their responsibilities to senior executives, lead to many variations in practice when it comes to:

- **Budget roles and responsibilities** – The exact role project managers play in creating budgets will vary.
- **What is included in budgets** – Some organizations include the reserves, others do not; some will require tracking of indirect expenses, and others will not.
- **How budgets are formatted** – Almost every organization has its unique budgeting format designed for senior management and the Finance Department.
- **Procurement practices vary greatly** –The variations often affect cost management practices.
- **Accuracy and precision of budgets** – Rules here vary considerably – one organization we know requires rounding to the nearest nickel, while most encourage whole numbers.
- **How to control costs and who controls them** – Control mechanisms and those with responsibility will vary.

It is incumbent on the project manager to consult with their management, Project Management Office (PMO), senior management, and finance professionals to ensure compliance with all applicable rules. Citing standards and best practices usually does not help create change.

CHAPTER 2

Chapter 2: The Time Value of Money

For projects, time is money. The money we have now is worth more than the same amount we may receive in the future. This principle, known as the Time Value of Money, holds that money today has the potential to earn a return and increase in value. This return informs project selection and planning.

Interest

Interest is paid to those who lend money and is received by those who borrow money or invest in other ways (e.g., by purchasing bonds). Simple interest is paid only on the principal (the amount originally borrowed). In contrast, compound interest is paid on the accumulated amount of both principal and interest.

The amount of interest paid is based on many factors, including:

- Availability of funds
- Economic conditions (e.g., inflation, government intervention, current interest rates)
- Assessment of ability to repay a loan

- Time of the loan
- Liquidity of the loan

Interest received on investment is called "return," and interest paid constitutes the cost of borrowing money. It is essential for project cost management when deciding which projects to initiate and how to fund them. Organizations may weigh whether to invest the funds or spend them on projects.

When interest rates on fixed investments are relatively low, investment in projects is encouraged. Investment in projects is encouraged, as a project may offer a higher return than saving money. Lower interest rates also mean borrowing for projects is a relatively inexpensive source of funding.

Dividends

Stocks (and alternative investments such as mutual funds) are another form of investment that can generate returns or raise capital for projects. A stock (also known as equity) is a form of security providing a fractional interest in the issuing company that is proportional to the amount invested. In addition, stocks pay dividends, typically quarterly, to investors. These returns are taken from corporate profits or reserves (i.e., money set aside to cover future obligations).

Unlike loans, which are typically for fixed rates, dividends can vary. Not all stocks pay dividends; however, all have the potential for growth in the stock market. A good average return on stock investments (growth and dividends) is considered 10% or more for comparative purposes.

Future Value

The future value (FV) is what an investment will be worth after a certain number of years. Suppose we invest $1,000 today at 12% compound interest. At the end of one year, the investment will be worth $1,000 + 0.12 × $1,000, or $1,120. At the end of the second year, it increases to $1,120 + 0.12 × $1,120, or $1,254.

In other words, calculate the future value as

$$FV = (1 + r)^n * PV$$

Equation 1: Future Value

where **r** is the interest rate, **n** is the number of periods, and **PV** is the present or current value.

The formula can include multiple rates over an arbitrary number of periods, such as months and years. In this case, the power of various financial calculation software applications (e.g., Excel) can assist with computations.

If all other factors are equal, favor projects with higher future values.

Present Value

Present value (PV) is the current value of funds expected in the future. A process known as discounting calculates the current worth. Assume, for example, that you will receive $1,254 in two years, including 12% interest compounded annually. Therefore, the present value must be less than $1,254, and it can be calculated by subtracting the 12% interest received. Remove the interest by calculating the discount rate[3], which is

$$\frac{1}{(1+r)^n}$$

and multiplying the future value by it. We can solve for the present value by

$$PV = \frac{1}{(1+r)^n} * FV$$

Equation 2: Present Value

where **FV** is the future value, **r** is the interest rate, and **n** is the number of periods.

Filling in the information, we find

$$PV = \frac{1}{(1+.12)^2} * 1{,}254$$

Applying appropriate rounding[4], we find

$$PV = .80 \times 1{,}254$$

Therefore, the present value is approximately $1,000.

---

[3] For present value computations, the discount rate is the sacrificed interest if an investor chose to accept an amount in the future as opposed to receiving and then investing the same amount today.

[4] See Appendix B for Rules of Rounding. If this were an accounting or finance text, values would not be rounded. Project management is not as concerned with precision, and rounding is usually appropriate.

Inflation

Inflation is a broad measure of the purchasing power of money. Inflation rates rise as prices of goods and services rise. Higher inflation reduces the purchasing power of money and the ability to fund projects.

Longer-term projects, lasting 5-10 years or more, should account for inflation. For example, one of the largest and most complex infrastructure projects undertaken in the US was Boston's Central Artery/Tunnel project, also known as the "Big Dig." The project spanned more than 20 years, with some subprojects lasting more than 10 years. Inflation accounted for a large portion of budget overruns throughout the project lifecycle.

The project's spending grew from US$2 billion to over US$ 14 billion. The spending increase was primarily due to unanticipated increases in labor and material costs. "It is claimed that a major cost escalation factor on the Big Dig was inflation on all project elements lasting more than a decade, and the project management team reported that about half of the cost growth was caused by inflation (Greiman & Warburton 2009)."

There have been periods when inflation has been historically low, often below 3%. However, project managers should not assume it will remain low throughout a project's life. Therefore, consider how salaries, fees, and other costs will increase and accumulate over time when estimating and budgeting longer projects.

Chapter Summary

Chapter 2 introduces the Time Value of Money, the idea that money today is worth more than the same amount in the future because it can earn a return. Interest, dividends, future value, and present value shape project funding decisions.

"The money we have now is worth more than the same amount we may receive in the future." Compound interest increases value over time, while discounting helps determine the present value of future funds. The chapter also highlights the impact of inflation, showing how rising costs, such as those seen in the Big Dig, can significantly affect long-term project budgets.

- **Formulas**: FV and PV

Knowledge Nuggets

Chapter Pro Tip: Time is Money for Projects

Time is money for projects. The money we have now is worth more than the same amount we may receive in the future. It also means that money received sooner is more valuable than the same amount received later. The value is because we can either invest money in projects or financial accounts and expect a further return.

Rather than putting all the eggs in one basket, organizations will invest in a variety of projects or investment vehicles to protect the value of their cash. While bank accounts in today's economy pay less than 1%, investments in stocks and bonds still yield 2%- 10% or more. As a result, project returns from successful products may also be higher.

The time value of money creates a natural tension in the economy. Investments can increase in value. However, long-term inflation can reduce buying power. Therefore, spending some cash now or spreading it out more evenly over time may be beneficial. If possible, this would also motivate buyers and sellers to hold some cash on hand.

Modern tools such as Google Sheets, MS Excel, and financial calculators will help ease the burden of computations formerly requiring interest tables. These tools and calculations are necessary for comparing potential projects.

Since time is money on projects, a project manager needs to minimize wasted time. The waste may range from padded estimates and schedules to “gold-plated” products (those which exceed scope and requirements) to ineffective communications.

Learn more about the forms of project waste and do your best to reduce or eliminate waste in your projects.

CHAPTER 3

Chapter 3: Principles and Best Practices for Success

Project managers need the most flexibility when managing project costs. Some may never have budget responsibilities, while others may have partial or complete responsibility. Those with some duties will need to navigate many organizational practices dealing with issues such as:

- Financial policies
- Estimating practices
- Costs needed or excluded
- Budget formats
- Accuracy requirements

It is often the project manager's responsibility to determine these requirements and ensure they are met. Therefore, it is essential to consult with your management, the Project Management Office (PMO), if one exists, or finance professionals to learn more about the requirements.

Here are six best practices that will help you achieve project success. They also apply to a wide range of cost management practices.

Cost Management is a Weakness

We know a project manager who recognized this weakness. He managed software projects with a salaried team. For much of his early career, management did not require a budget. With no budget responsibilities, he studied accounting and finance, gaining a deeper understanding of how his organization managed its budgets.

One day, management asked him to determine and manage the budget for a project undertaken to upgrade the networking infrastructure of all corporate facilities. Had he not been prepared, he might not have been given the assignment. To his surprise, this assignment became a gateway to managing a much larger program later.

Project cost management is an essential component of project management. However, many project managers have little to no exposure to budgets in early assignments. If you are one of these project managers, you need to acquire this essential skill. Although you will not need and are not expected to possess all this knowledge, map out a learning plan spanning over a year or more. In addition, it may be necessary to revisit some of this learning to adopt new practices during the transition to a new organization.

Your Budget is Only an Estimate

Keep in mind that your budget is not absolute but rather only an estimate. It does not need to be precise (e.g., $1,100,456.35) and only needs to be within a specified accuracy (e.g., ±25 %). You will probably revise your budget a few times before project execution. With each iteration, you will get closer to the final amount. A common expectation is that the project's actual expense will be within 5-10% of the budgeted amount.

Where budget items are quantifiable, do the math and use the result. Also include all expenses, such as fees, taxes (if applicable), and costs. Long-term projects may also need to consider the effect of inflation. After that, good estimating processes will help you arrive at an achievable budget.

A rate card specifies what an organization is willing to pay for specific resources. For example, Human Resources may publish salary or cost-to-company rate cards for particular titles and roles. Alternatively, a government agency may issue a rate card specifying the maximum amount it is willing to pay for specific materials. Determine whether rate cards can provide estimates or constrain resource allocation.

When we say "the budget is only an estimate," it also means you can drop the "cents" when discussing or presenting the budget to anyone. Knowledge and application of sound rounding rules are also critical.

You Do Not Always Get What You Want

Remember that the budget amount specified in the project charter can constrain some organizations. Therefore, you must reconcile the estimated budget with that constraint.

Recall the story of the project manager we started talking about earlier in this chapter? When management considered the project's budget, they contacted vendors and received quotes ranging from $1 million to $1.5 million and higher. However, they had not initially allocated any funds to the project, so they decided to go in-house.

The first task for the newly assigned project manager was to develop a budget. Working with a consultant who helped design the project, he reduced the cost to $300,000. Management was pleased but challenged him to reduce it to $250,000.

The project manager returned to the team and asked for alternative designs and approaches to the work. They found they could comfortably accommodate $250,000, but could not go any lower without making severe sacrifices. Management considered the rationale the project manager presented and approved the project manager's continued participation, along with a promotion to program management.

Integrate with Other Performance Domain Processes

To develop a successful budget, at a minimum, the scope and schedule are required. Their related processes will provide timeframes and costs to be factored into cost estimates and budgets. In addition, risk management will provide data needed to develop contingency reserves appropriately.

While these are the most common touchpoints, there may be more. For example, if a project requires a public relations campaign, the cost of communications management should be included in the project cost. Similarly, if procurement is involved, printing costs for a Request for Proposal may be required[5]. Therefore, as part of the budgeting process, review each performance domain carefully to identify any additional costs.

Your New Best Friend

As a project manager, you lead by influence, not manage by authority. Estimating costs is challenging. For example, the Human Resources department will not provide you with specific people's salaries. Still, you may need to use some internal resources for your project. Some material costs may also be challenging to estimate.

Your organization's cost accountant can become your new best friend in these circumstances. Their job is to analyze costs, and they can often answer questions others cannot. For example, they may not disclose the exact salary for the programmer or electrician your project needs. Still, they can tell you their average cost. Then, when you complete your budget, they will also be one of the best experts to review it.

Check Variance Weekly

Some organizations may only require a status report to be submitted fortnightly or monthly. Do not wait for the status report to review your budget variance (i.e., the amount you are over or under budget at any point in the project); review it weekly. Checking at this frequency will reduce the time required to identify an issue, develop a solution, and confirm that the solution works.

---

[5] Procurement, once a Knowledge Area, is now listed in the PMBOK Guide as a "complementary discipline," rather than a performance domain.

The interval will often also help reduce the severity of adjustments needed to get back on track with the budget.

In addition, you will need to monitor any trends in variance. For example, has the cost overrun been increasing week after week? Did you detect any big spike (outlier)? These conditions indicate the need to analyze the situation carefully and determine whether any corrective actions are required.

Chapter Summary

Chapter 3 outlines six best practices that help project managers succeed in cost management. The chapter emphasizes that many project managers begin with limited budgeting experience. Because of this, developing financial literacy and building a long-term learning plan is essential.

Budgets are estimates, not precise figures, and should fall within acceptable ranges of accuracy. Budgets are not absolutes, but estimates. Rounding and rate cards are among the practical tools for building realistic numbers.

Project managers must often work within constraints and may need to adjust scope or design to meet funding limits. Successful budgeting requires integrating information from other performance domains (e.g., governance, scope, schedule, risk, communications, and stakeholders) and from disciplines (e.g., procurement) to ensure that all costs are captured.

A key relationship is with the cost accountant, who can provide critical cost insights even when specific salary or pricing details cannot be shared. Finally, the chapter advises reviewing budget variance weekly, not just during formal reporting cycles, to catch trends early and take corrective action before issues escalate.

Knowledge Nuggets

Chapter Pro Tip: Ensure all agreed-upon changes include financial impacts, including those from new risks, and track them separately until there is agreement to rebaseline.

Any changes to a project's scope may also impact time, resources, and costs, the traditional project constraints. Before signing off on or declining a change request, analyze its impact thoroughly. In addition to potential new fixed costs, some resources, including their operation costs, may be needed for a longer period.

It is also good to track and report these cost changes separately from your budget. First, it helps create a feedback loop for stakeholders to visualize the impact of requested changes. Then fold these changes into the budget during re-planning and re-baselining.

Finally, changes also need to be examined for risks. Any single change is usually not a good reason to change the contingency reserve amount. However, if there are many changes, a review may be necessary.

PART II: CREATING AND FUNDING THE BUDGET (INITIATION THROUGH PLANNING)

"It is easy to launch a project if you have no clue about the cost and schedule."

— **Gerry Geek**

CHAPTER 4

Chapter 4: Project Selection Techniques Using Cost

Cost is a critical factor in deciding which projects to initiate and plan further. Therefore, obtaining cost estimates as accurately as possible will ensure the business can begin projects aligned with its strategy promptly.

Note that cost should not be the only factor. For example, a new product may be necessary to maintain a competitive advantage. Organizations will need to develop project selection criteria that work best for them and their projects.

A sound portfolio management system provides a single, integrated solution to ensure the optimal mix of projects is always in place. The optimal blend should ensure the organization continuously improves, remains flexible, and does more with less funding.

Once we have determined that a project will move forward, we should create a project charter. This project charter should state the high-level scope, budget, and resources, and provide more detail as needed. In addition, the project charter should name the project manager responsible for delivering the project. In many smaller projects, particularly in consulting or when time-and-materials contracts are used, we may use a more detailed contract in addition to the project charter.

The Project Business Case

A project business case is an essential document that aggregates and communicates the information and knowledge needed to develop a portfolio, program, or project charter. In addition, a business case should identify the project's value and benefits for the project team and other stakeholders.

A business case should be considered a "living document," revisable as more information about the project becomes known. Depending on findings from detailed planning, some components may need to be updated or refreshed. The business case should also be periodically reviewed and compared with project progress to ensure the project's promised benefits are delivered.

Often, the organization undertaking the project will have its own ideas of content and outline. The following paragraphs will outline some key content.

First, the business case should document the selected project or opportunity. Analysis of that problem or opportunity should include:

- How the solution contributes to and aligns with business goals
- The root causes of the pain or opportunity
- All the supporting analysis developed while examining the current and future state and identifying the gaps

- A highlight or summary of these gaps and the deliverables meant to satisfy them.

The business case also needs to contain information about the alternatives considered. The information developed may include assumptions and constraints, dependencies, valuations, and financial analysis to support decision-making and establish an initial budget and timeline.

Once the alternatives are laid out, there should be a clear recommendation. The proposal should include the analysis and rationale for the selected option(s), a cost-benefit analysis, high-level milestones, and a product map, any dependencies between the proposed work and existing work, and the roles and responsibilities needed to carry out the project.

Finally, the business case should provide evaluation information – how will we measure the project and know that:

- The resulting work conforms to all requirements,
- The resulting work is fit for use,
- The delivered product meets or exceeds expectations, and
- The promised benefits have been achieved.

Depending on your organization, other key content may be required, such as:

- Market and economic analysis
- Organizational needs and customer requests
- Strategic opportunities
- Technological advances expected
- Legal, environmental, regulatory, or other compliance required
- Social needs

Checklists and Scoring Models

Performing high-level or detailed screens requires a checklist or scoring model to ensure that all potential projects are evaluated against uniform criteria. However, checklists may be adequate for smaller, more straightforward projects. Checklists list the necessary, agreed-upon decision criteria and provide a qualitative scoring method (e.g., good, better, best).

Smaller organizations may use checklists to determine if the project cost management elements are appropriate for initiation. The list may include items such as:

- Initial cost estimated
- Budget and resources are available
- Project meets a strategic need
- Future profitability has been analyzed

Larger, higher-risk projects might include more detail and assign weights to criteria using a more granular, quantitative scale to ensure a thorough analysis. Once the items are scored, potential projects are compared. Those that best meet the financial and non-financial criteria should move ahead.

Cost-Benefit Analysis

Cost-benefit analysis (CBA) or the Cost-Benefit Ratio (CBR) is excellent for comparing a project with alternatives that share similar goals. We may also compare a new project with our current operations. Each alternative solution is evaluated based on the resources required and the projected benefits.

Determining the costs and benefits will require a detailed analysis to ensure we account for all factors. Suppose we are evaluating imaging solutions to replace our paper documents. Examples of costs for our paper-based system include paper, file folders, cabinets, storage space, personnel time to manage paper and storage, and copy machines. The scanning solution would include costs for scanners and computers, storage media, housing for computer equipment, and personnel to operate the equipment. We need to brainstorm these potential costs.

Divide benefits into “hard” dollar benefits (measurable) and “soft” dollar benefits (non-financial or other benefits that are challenging to measure). For example, a hard-dollar benefit of our scanning solution might be the savings from avoiding the costs of searching for lost documents. Compute the cost by determining the average time spent searching for lost documents and the personnel costs for the search. A soft benefit might be the modern, up-to-date appearance we present to potential customers visiting our facilities, which could drive more sales.

Once we have identified all costs and hard-dollar benefits, we can develop a ratio. Then, suppose two projects have similar proportions. In that case, we can consider soft benefits and other factors in making our selection. Finally, if the cost-benefit ratio and payback period are favorable, perhaps we should proceed with the project.

Looking at the ratio alone is usually insufficient, since two projects may have the same ratio but differ in cost by millions. We therefore need to ensure the selected projects fit our budgets. We also need to be very careful to make sure we have included all the highest costs and benefits. It is often helpful to have a business analyst conduct the CBA and have a third party review the analysis to ensure an independent review.

Total Cost of Ownership

Cost-benefit analysis typically focuses on current project costs and future benefits. In contrast, Total Cost of Ownership (TCO) encompasses all costs associated with delivering the solution and its operating costs over its lifetime. While some projects may be less expensive to produce, their future operational costs may be prohibitive.

The typical lifespan of software and technology-related projects is three to five years. If you are uncertain about the time, discussing the project with an accountant who handles depreciation would be beneficial, as the useful life is closely tied to depreciation.

For each period, deduct any hard dollar benefits or expected revenues from the accumulated costs to derive the ownership costs for each period. As with cost-benefit analysis, soft-dollar benefits can support it.

Cost Metrics

Cost metrics can inform project selection and cost management planning about project value. However, it is essential to note that cost should not be the only criterion. This section presents commonly used metrics for evaluating and comparing projects. Is there one best? Unfortunately, not even experts agree.

Return on Assets (ROA). Return on Assets determines how efficiently assets are used to generate a profit. Expressed as a percentage, a higher ROA is preferable. For example, 10% ROA means that for every dollar of assets, $0.10 profit is generated.

$$ROA = \frac{Net\ Income}{Total\ Assets}\ x\ 100\%$$

Equation 3: Return on Assets

Return on Average Capital Employed (ROACE). Return on average capital employed measures the efficiency of profitability. It is particularly useful for analyzing capital-intensive industries like oil refining. Because it uses average capital over time, it can account for seasonal fluctuations in business.

$$ROACE = \frac{Earning\ Before\ Interest\ and\ Taxes}{Average\ Capital\ Employed}$$

Equation 4: Return on Average Capital Employed

Average Capital Employed is typically the mean of the opening and closing capital employed over a period.

Return on Investment (ROI). Return on Investment is used to estimate the probability of a gain or loss on an investment. It compares the investment gain to the actual investment.

$$ROI = \frac{Investment\ Gain}{Investment}\ x\ 100\%$$

Equation 5: Return on Investment

If we invest $1 and estimate we will earn $1, then the return on investment is 100%.

$$ROI = \frac{1}{1}\ x\ 100\% = 100\%$$

A higher-ROI investment is preferred. However, one issue with the ROI metric is that it does not account for the time value of money. Therefore, Net Present Value (NPV) is more commonly used to compare projects.

Net Present Value (NPV). The NPV is similar to the present value, but it accounts for both costs and future cash flows. If t is the period and T is the total number of periods, then

$$NPV = \sum_{t=1}^{T} \frac{Cash\ in - Cash\ out\ during\ t}{(1+r)^t}$$

OR

$$NPV = \sum_{t=1}^{t} PV_t - Investment$$

Equation 6: Net Present Value

Therefore, projects with higher NPV and positive NPV are more desirable and should influence portfolio selection.

The PMP® exam typically focuses on the second form of the formula. An example problem might be:

> A small construction project with an expected cost of $1 million will generate $5 million (in terms of present value) over ten years. What is the NPV?
>
> **Solution**:
>
> NPV – Investment = $5 million - $1 million = $4 million

Internal Rate of Return (IRR). The internal rate of return measures the profitability of investments. IRR is the discount rate,[6] (r), that would make the Net Present Value equal 0. Therefore, substitute 0 for the NPV and solve for r in the above equation. Given the solution's complexity, it is best to calculate NPV and IRR using a tool such as Microsoft Excel, which has built-in NPV and IRR functions.

Payback Period (PP). The payback period is the time required to recoup the project's cost (excluding the time value of money). Therefore,

$$PP = \frac{Investment}{Annual\ Net\ Cash\ Flow}$$

Equation 7: Payback Period

Suppose $1,000 is invested in a project. If the product generates $500 in annual revenue for two years, the project's payback period is two years.

$$PP = \frac{1{,}000}{500} = 2$$

Shorter payback times are preferred because they free up funding to start additional projects more quickly.

Opportunity Cost (OC). Opportunity cost is about the "sacrifices made to gain some benefit (Pyle & Larson 1981)." While these costs are not formally recognized in accounting, consider them when evaluating projects. For example, suppose we want to invest $1

---

[6] "The discount rate will be company-specific as it is related to how the company gets its funds. It is the rate of return that the investors expect or the cost of borrowing money. If shareholders expect a 12% return, that is the discount rate the company will use to calculate NPV (Gallo 2014). "

million in a project to improve plant and equipment. Unfortunately, we need to reject that project to invest $2m in a new product and remain competitive. In this case, $1m is the opportunity cost of implementing the project to remain competitive.

Total Project vs. Portfolio Cost Risk

"When managing costs, we need to understand that underperforming projects may result in losses for the project and the portfolio. In the worst-case scenario, the company may fail if one or more projects fail. In the best case, the project adds value to the portfolio and another project. For example, a failing software project may provide code that another project can reuse. Alternatively, this may mean using an architectural drawing with minor modifications for another construction project.

Total portfolio risk is often referred to as beta or systemic risk. There is a systemic risk arising from project interactions. We need to understand that a high project risk does not necessarily mean a high portfolio risk. Let us look at a couple of examples.

Suppose an oil and gas exploration company has several projects to consider for drilling wells. The basics of each project include:

- The cost of drilling a well is $2 million
- The probability of success is low – 10%
- Successful wells produce $24 million in revenue
- Unsuccessful wells are a 100% loss – ($2 million)

Here we can see that if we drill a well, we could lose up to 100% of our investment if no oil or gas is found. We also see a low probability of success – only a 10% chance that our well will be successful.

However, successful wells are enormous moneymakers. So, in this case, if we drill 100 wells, there is a high probability we will be profitable.

Expected Return = Expected Profit Per Well / Investment Required Per Well

=((Success Probability x Profit) + (Failure Probability x Loss)) /Investment Required Per Well

= ((.10 x 24 million) + (.90 x -2 million))/2 million

=.30 or 30%

Doing the math, we see there is an expected 30% return. Therefore, high project risk does not necessarily translate into high portfolio risk. It is also true that as we diversify our portfolio, we can reduce risk, much as we do with financial investments. Further, risks that are not market-related typically do not affect the portfolio risk.

Now let us consider another, less calculated example. A grocery store typically has low beta risk (everyone needs to eat), but wants to diversify by opening a computer store that sells computers to small businesses. So, what are the project and beta risks in general terms?

Here, we have a high level of project risk. A grocery store would have no expertise in the new business, and there are many competitors (e.g., Dell, Lenovo, HP).

There is also a much higher market risk. The new business would be more susceptible to economic changes. Suppose the new company fails or incurs a significant loss. In that case, it could begin to erode revenue from the core grocery business. So there is both high project risk and high beta risk in this case.

The Importance of a Basis for Initiation Estimates

Thriving, growing organizations have an ongoing need for projects. Therefore, estimated cash needs must be as accurate as possible. Also, there should be a basis for initiation estimates to achieve estimate accuracy.

Senior management must understand the need for accuracy. Any form of "padding" or addition of non-essential project elements should be discouraged at project initiation. Set aside project politics.

Consider if a manager at a prominent company made the following statement:

"I am so excited! I needed $2 million for all my projects. I requested $3.5 million and got $2.2 million. So I have $200,000 to play with this year (Morris 2010)!"

This attitude will delay other critical projects within the organization. Having transparency in financial processes is vital to organizational success. Trust needs to be built between the boardroom and senior executives.

It is equally important to have a basis for projects completed for clients. One organization we are familiar with learned this the hard way. Both the organization and its client were large, multinational organizations.

A division of the client company called their local sales office for a quote. There was interest across the company in the purchase. Upon learning this, the headquarters called their local sales office to provide a quote for the same acquisition. The quote provided to the client headquarters was more than double the division's quote.

The salespeople preparing quotes reviewed their quotas and used them to estimate each case. Now they were trapped. They could not explain rationally how the quotes were generated, and they lost tens of millions in sales. An estimating tool was developed to help salespeople explain why quotes may differ across offices, preventing additional lost sales.

Chapter Summary

Chapter 4 explains how organizations use cost-based techniques to select the right projects for their portfolios. While cost is important, cost should not be the only factor, since strategic alignment, competitiveness, and long-term value also matter. A strong portfolio management system helps maintain the optimal mix of projects.

The project business case is a "living document" that captures the problem or opportunity, alternatives, assumptions, constraints, financial analysis, and the rationale for the recommended solution. It also defines how success will be measured to ensure promised benefits are delivered.

Several project selection tools are introduced, including checklists, scoring models, cost-benefit analysis, total cost of ownership, and financial metrics such as ROA, ROACE, ROI, NPV, IRR, payback period, and opportunity cost. These tools help compare alternatives and determine which projects provide the greatest value.

A key insight is that project risk and portfolio risk differ. High project risk does not necessarily translate into high portfolio risk, especially when diversification reduces exposure. The chapter closes by stressing the importance of accurate initiation estimates and warns against "padding" budgets, which undermines trust and can delay other critical projects.

- **Formulas**: ROA, ROACE, ROI, NPV, IRR, PP, OC

Knowledge Nuggets

Chapter Template: Project Business Case Template, Cost-Benefit Analysis Template

Chapter Pro Tip: When choosing projects to initiate and add to a portfolio, do not focus exclusively on costs.

Design and initiate projects to implement a strategy. As such, it is essential to understand non-financial reasons for projects. Focusing solely on costs may adversely affect strategy, for example, by producing poor-quality products or failing to meet a critical operational requirement.

Some non-financial reasons to initiate projects may include, but are not limited to, projects necessary to:

- Sustain or grow operations
- Remain competitive
- Increase efficiency and productivity
- Meet diverse stakeholder needs
- Refresh aging facilities or products

Costs are an excellent tool for choosing between similar alternatives. A lower-cost project may be the best alternative if all other factors are equal. Lower-cost projects may also enable the initiation of additional projects and help keep the organization within budget.

CHAPTER 5

CHAPTER 5: FINANCE PERFORMANCE PLANNING

Complete detailed planning once a project is initiated. Careful planning typically starts with a project plan that includes sections for each project management performance domain, including financial performance.

The Cost Management Plan is not the estimates or the budget (except for minor projects), but rather a description of how to formulate them. When the document is complete, the team will know the essentials for being good financial stewards of their projects.

What is a Cost Management Plan?

The purpose of the project management plan, and hence the financial management plan, is to help the project manager guide the team to success. The plan establishes the procedures, methods, and measures for planning, managing, spending, and controlling project costs.

The best financial management plans are project-sized and reusable. So, rather than reiterating policy found elsewhere, either add value to it or refer to it. Generally, writing a solid cost management plan for your first project will give you a reusable template for future projects.

Critical Financial Management Plan Topics

For a complete financial management plan, consider the following sections (also in the financial management plan template) for a comprehensive plan that is appropriate for all but minor projects:

Documentation

- **Title, Date, Author** – identifies the document and who is responsible for it
- **Document Control Information** – identifies updates to the document, when it was updated, by whom, and the updates made
- **Table of Contents** – where to find information in the document
- **Purpose of the Document** – brief statement of goals for the document

Governance

- **Roles and Responsibilities** – who will be involved in the cost management processes and areas of responsibility
- **Cost Management Approach** – a summary of the steps to be taken to create the cost management plan and how to establish and update the cost baseline

Estimation and Budget

- **Cost Estimating** – information about how costs will be identified and documented, including
    - Techniques to be used
    - Work location(s)
    - Units of measurement
    - Accuracy and precision required
- **Budget** – how the budget will be created and reported, including
    - **Format** – how the budget will be formatted
    - **Currency** – the currency the budget will be in (best practice is that the budget should be in a single currency)
    - **Costs** – how to determine them from the estimates and the categories that identify them
    - **Reserves** – which reserves are included or excluded

Technology and Versioning

- **Estimation and Budgeting Technology** – what software and other technology will be used to estimate and display the budget, answering questions such as:
    - **Storage** – where the budget and related documentation are stored
    - **Access permissions** – who can read and modify the budget and related documentation
    - **Version control** – how is the budget and related documentation versioned

Monitoring, Controlling, and Reporting

- **Baselining** – when and how will baselines be created and used; when and how is rebaselining performed

- **Performance Measures and Rules –** how will budget performance be measured
    - **Rules for computing % complete –** how do we determine completion
    - **Specification of Earned Value methods –** which Earned Value methods are used
    - **Metrics –** what metrics will be maintained
    - **Tolerance for variance –** variance requiring action
    - **Rules for contingency and management reserve –** how reserves are managed
- **Cost Control** – techniques for controlling project costs, including
    - How to track expenditures
    - How cost variance is measured, and at what frequency
    - How to treat unacceptable variance
    - Reporting formats and frequencies
    - Accuracy and precision of reports and other cost control measures
- **Cost Change Control –** how to make changes to the cost management plan and related documents (e.g., estimates, budgets)

End Matter

- **Plan Approvals –** signatures of critical stakeholders to record buy-in
- **Glossary –** definition of terms and abbreviations
- **Appendices –** copies of any forms used and other supplemental information

Other Plan Topics

Almost no template is ready to use "off the shelf." While the critical topics are necessary for virtually all projects, some areas may be project- or industry-specific. These projects may benefit from some of the following sections (and this is not an exhaustive list):

- **Prospectus** – a summary of project finances and financial benefits for senior executives and investors
- **Basis of Estimate (BoE)** – may supplement or replace some information in the cost management plan if a BoE was created (see chapter, Cost Estimation Techniques, for more details)
- **Tables of Rates and Costs** – if they exist, these could be inserted into appendices
- **Capital Budgeting** – how to handle capital budget items, including their acquisition and depreciation or amortization
- **Insurance or Bonding Requirements** – document any policies or bonds required
- **Resources to be Purchased or Procured** – any information needed for buyers or procurement specialists in your organization (detailed requirements may be in separate documents or appendices of the cost management plan)
- **Financing Requirements** – documentation of loans, including repayment terms and any bonds issued, including dividend schedules
- **Escalation Procedures –** when and to whom financial issues must be escalated
- **Integration Points with Other Plans –** describes the interactions between the financial performance domain and the other six domains

- **Quality- Related Practices –** peer review requirements, financial audits, and checklists; may be provided by a Project Management Office (PMO)
- **Risk-Related Budgeting Practices –** how budget risks are identified, and reserves are managed; may be included in the Risk Management Plan
- **Budget Freeze Periods –** Times when a budget may not be modified; applicable in highly regulated or controlled environments
- **Vendor and Third-Party Budgeting Requirements –** especially useful for projects with procurements and outsourcing

Chapter Summary

Chapter 5 explains how to develop a cost management plan once a project has been initiated. The chapter emphasizes that the plan is not the estimates or the budget, but rather a description of how to formulate them, guiding the team in responsible cost stewardship.

A Cost Management Plan defines the procedures, methods, and measures for planning, managing, and controlling project costs. Strong plans are scalable, reusable, and aligned with organizational policy rather than duplicating it.

The chapter outlines the critical components of a complete financial management plan, including governance roles, estimating methods, budgeting formats, reserve strategies, technology and version control, baselining, earned value rules, variance thresholds, and cost-control procedures. As the text notes, these elements ensure the team knows "how to track expenditures," manage variance, and maintain accuracy.

Additional optional sections may be needed depending on the project or industry, such as capital budgeting, procurement requirements, financing terms, risk-related budgeting, or vendor-specific rules. Because no template fits all situations, project managers must tailor the plan to the project's context while ensuring completeness and clarity.

Knowledge Nuggets

Chapter Template: Project Cost Management Plan Template

Chapter Pro Tip: A good cost management plan can help with edits to other projects.

Spending time writing a good cost management plan can be valuable. A cost management plan includes many items that are not going to change over time or projects within an organization, such as:

- Estimation techniques to be used
- Budget policies, procedures, and formats
- Cost control methods
- Change control

Take the time on your first project to develop a plan, and then edit and reuse it for future projects. This strategy will save time while ensuring continued financial success for projects.

CHAPTER 6

CHAPTER 6: COST ESTIMATION TECHNIQUES

An estimate is an assessment of a quantitative result expressed in units. Estimates should indicate their precision or confidence. Most importantly, estimates are best described as ranges that reflect the uncertainty inherent in project planning (PMI 2001). For example, an estimate of a project's total cost might be USD 536 million ± USD $50 million at 90% confidence.

It is better to count, measure, and compute – it gets the best possible result. However, there is always uncertainty in estimation, and no single answer is correct. Therefore, we often derive estimates using rough calculations, explicit assumptions, or rules of thumb. For example, with assumptions and rules of thumb:

- Professional contractors hired for home improvements often provide quotes in dollars per square foot based on experience.
- Research has shown that computer programmers can produce ten debugged lines of code per day, regardless of the programming language used.

Reasonable estimates combine professional experience and judgment with independent expert reviews. Use multiple approaches and estimators before merging the results into a final estimate. Estimation is a "team sport" – more heads in the game are better than one, fostering collaboration and confidence.

Estimates require validation. Use tools and techniques not used to create the estimate to validate it. These may include a rule of thumb, industry allocation methods, checks against historical data, or expert opinions on the estimate. Once validated, it would be appropriate to save the estimate with the details of how it was derived and validated.

Top-Down vs. Bottom-Up

Top-down estimates lack details on categories or on how estimated time and money will be used. These will likely need to be broken down and detailed later. These estimates are typically developed for project initiation by senior executives or others, based on historical data, rules of thumb, or professional judgment.

A top-down estimate may also be a rough order-of-magnitude or "ballpark" estimate. These estimates are expected to have the same accuracy as initiation estimates (i.e., -25% to +75% of the actual). However, in addition to project initiation, such estimates may help validate more detailed estimates (i.e., they are in the right ballpark).

Bottom-up estimates assess the lowest level of detail of the Work Breakdown Structure, usually the work packages. Then aggregate the estimates for each work package to obtain initial project time and cost estimates.

Bottom-up estimates are usually best determined by counting, measuring, and making reasonable assumptions. For example, if a project hires a contractor paid $50 per hour to perform 2 hours of work, the contractor is estimated to cost $100.

A critical risk of bottom-up estimation is the omission of work packages. Accurately determining all work packages at the beginning of a project is difficult, if not impossible. However, ignoring a busy or costly work package will make the estimate inaccurate. Therefore, it is crucial to consider this risk when computing reserves.

There are times when other techniques are needed. Three standard estimation techniques to obtain a detailed estimate are:

Parametric estimates. Parametric estimates use historical data and statistics to determine costs. For example, suppose we are estimating the time required for a computer programming task. The developers estimate the job will require 100 lines of code based on a statistical analysis of past work. They are paid an aggregate of $1,000 per day. Based on research showing developers can produce 10 lines of debugged code per day, the estimated cost is 100/10 x 1,000 = $10,000, and the developers complete in 10 days.

Analogous estimates. Analogous estimates use expert judgment to apply information from similar past projects to form an estimate. For example, a project manager is estimating the time and cost to have an architect design a small home. The architect's rate is $400 per hour. Last month, the architect designed a similar structure in two days for $6,400. The architect confirms that a similar design strategy and scope of work are required for the new home. Therefore, the project manager estimates a duration of 2 days and a cost of $6,400.

3-point estimates. Also known as a triangular distribution, 3-point estimation uses three data points to compute an average. The three points are the optimistic (O), pessimistic (P), and most likely (M) estimates. Parametric or analogous estimates, expert judgment, or any other means may determine these three points. The three points are added together and then divided by 3.

$$\text{Cost estimate} = (O+P+M) / 3$$

Equation 8: Triangular Distribution or 3-Point Estimate

For example, if the time a $50 per hour contractor will work is uncertain, suppose the contractor suggests that:

Best case, the work is completed in an hour ($50),

Likely case, the work will take two hours ($100), and

Worst case, the contractor might complete it in four hours ($150)

In this case, our schedule estimate is (1 + 2 + 4)/3 = 2.33 days (or 2 days when rounded appropriately), and our cost estimate is ($ 50 + $100 + $150)/3 = $100.

Program and Evaluation Review Technique (PERT)

The US Navy, working with Booz Allen Hamilton, developed the Program Evaluation and Review Technique, or PERT, in the late 1950s. The goal was to improve the management of more than 10,000 contractors on the Polaris missile project (Wikipedia 2021). The emphasis of PERT is on controlling the schedule using flexible costs. Its benefit is that it provides, in mathematical form, everything an estimate should include: a range and a confidence level.

The basis of PERT estimation is the development of a weighted average using the most likely, optimistic, and pessimistic estimates. PERT estimates, also known as Beta distributions, are superior to triangular distributions, which can overweight pessimistic and optimistic estimates. PERT is well-suited to innovative projects that manage risk by providing more precise estimates.

The fundamental PERT formula is the sum of the pessimistic (P), four times the most likely (M), and optimistic (O) estimates, divided by six. Finally, calculate the results for each task in the schedule and sum them.

To assess the estimate's range and confidence, we need to examine its standard deviation. The standard deviation for each task is calculated by subtracting the optimistic (O) value from the pessimistic (P) value, then dividing the difference by 6. While the reason is too complex for anything but an advanced statistics course, we cannot add the standard deviations. Instead, we look at the variance. Variance is equal to the standard deviation squared. (Note that statistical variance is unrelated to the other project management usage of "variance" as the difference between plan and actual.) When we sum the variances and take the square root, we get the standard deviation needed for the range.

The confidence level is 1 standard deviation, approximately 68%. So, if we double the square root of the variances, we have a confidence level of two standard deviations.

To summarize, to complete the PERT estimate, we need to find the weighted average and variance for each task, then sum the weighted estimates. The range, positive or negative, will be the square root of the sum of the variances.

Suppose we double the square root of the sum of the variances. In that case, we now have the result for two standard deviations and are about 95% confident in the interval. In general, a 95% confidence level is sufficient for most projects. When n is the number of tasks to estimate, the PERT formula is

$$Cost\ estimate = \sum_{i=1}^{n} \frac{P + O + 4 * M}{6} \pm 2\left(\sqrt{\sum_{i=1}^{n}\left(\frac{P - O}{6}\right)^2}\right)$$

Equation 9: PERT Estimation with 95% Confidence

Please see Appendix C: More About PERT for a complete example and a guide to using PERT to answer estimate "what if" questions.

Modern Estimation Methods

Modern estimating techniques have evolved to improve the accuracy of core estimating methods through technological advances or to increase estimating efficiency. For example, many estimating models have been developed for specific industries and projects. For software, there is COCOMO II; for construction, models such as ProSwift and STACK. Some models typically bypass best practices for developing a WBS and performing bottom-up estimating; therefore, they must be carefully selected to align with specific project circumstances.

As artificial intelligence moves into mainstream projects, it may be used to augment analogous, top-down, or parametric estimates by combing through data from hundreds of projects. It is, however, not sufficient for the estimator to ask for an estimate. Proper prompts are necessary to provide context and other essential information.

One standard prompt is the RTF (Role, Task, Format) format. An example prompt may include:

> **Role:** Expert and experienced estimator of construction projects.
>
> **Task:** Estimate the time and cost to build a new home. The architectural diagrams, project scope statement, and WBS will be uploaded. Check our company archive for information on past projects. If necessary, request any additional inputs required before beginning the task. Use all available information to determine the time required to complete construction.
>
> **Output:** Provide a table listing tasks and resources, along with time and cost estimates, to complete the project.

The best-constructed prompts will also consider the formats most suitable for the AI model in use. All output from an AI estimate needs to be scrutinized for validity. Further prompts may also be required to clarify information, request additional breakdowns, or otherwise iterate until a level of comfort with the estimate is achieved.

Function point analysis (FPA) is another effective method for estimating when sufficient experience with repetitive work is available. It may be used to estimate specific resources and circumstances or, in some cases, the entire project. Scanning the internet for articles on Function Point Analysis reveals a near-exclusive focus on software. However, there are many possible applications if considered in its simplest form, where work is divided into repeatable units.

FPA divides the work into approximately identical, repeatable units. Examples are easily found in software and construction:

- Framing and drywalling the rooms of a home
- Writing functions or subroutines
- Laying carpet or painting
- Installing network components
- Configuring software using certain allowable operations

Home improvement contractors will quote their work in dollars per square foot. Based on their experience with the average home, they know how much wood, carpet, and other materials are used in a typical home improvement project. Their knowledge will allow them to estimate time and cost based on the total square footage.

For example, suppose an average builder takes 1 day to frame a 14-foot wall and ½ day to frame a 6-foot wall. The project will require 10 14-foot walls and 6 6-foot walls. The estimated time is then (10 x 1) + (6 x ½) = 13 days.

Estimation Accuracy

Accurately estimating project time and cost is critical for project management success. Without a clear understanding of time and costs, projects are prone to budget overruns, delays, and compromised quality. Whether managing a small-scale initiative or a multi-million-dollar endeavor, estimation is a skill that can make or break a project.

Every project should be estimated at least twice. Typically, an initial or sales estimate is developed using top-down estimation at project initiation. Another good time to estimate is during project planning. Once detailed requirements are known, the high-level design is complete, or a detailed project schedule is available, perform another estimate. Additional estimates ensure that significant changes to scope, schedule, cost, or resources that arise during planning are accounted for. The general expectations for estimating accuracy are as follows:

- Initiation estimate: -25% - +75% of actual
- Planning estimate: -10% - +25% of actual
- Definitive estimate before execution: -5% - +10% of actual (PMI 2017)

To be successful, develop an estimating process, follow it diligently, and include a review step. The following outlines a brief six-step framework for estimating that builds confidence and a sense of control.

Define. Start by defining the purpose and scope (i.e., what needs to be estimated) of the estimation. Clarifying these details enhances preparedness and reduces uncertainty, thereby making the process more transparent and trustworthy.

Collect. Be sure to collect input from all relevant sources, including subject-matter and industry experts with deep knowledge of the project. Other sources include the project plan, which lists the required resources to improve estimation accuracy. When resource availability is unknown, ensure that the project's overall size and scope are understood. In addition, gather relevant information and historical estimates from past projects.

Estimate. Prepare the baseline estimate. Consider all activities, tasks, resources, and costs. Choose the best estimation method (e.g., bottom-up, PERT) for each item to meet project accuracy requirements.

Analyze. No project operates in a risk-free environment. Identifying potential risks and their impact is a vital part of estimation. Common risks include market fluctuations, supply chain disruptions, scope changes, and unknown performance of resources. Incorporating contingency funds into a schedule and budget provides a buffer against unexpected time and expense costs. If accuracy is essential for a project, analyze risk information (e.g., the Estimated Monetary Value or EMV) to determine appropriate contingency reserves. Consult management for management reserves.

Validate. Review and check estimates. For example, bottom-up estimates may be checked by rules of thumb, reviewed by experts, or re-estimated by another team. Include time to adjust plans and, if necessary, to replan part of the project. Perhaps the most difficult challenge is maintaining environmental awareness of project dependencies for work outside the project. Estimates also need buy-in from all stakeholders, from the executive sponsor to project team members, to succeed. Buy-in keeps everyone aligned and working together toward project success.

Post-Estimate. Once the estimates are complete or have been revised, review and update the budget. Also, assign the appropriate resources to the project, with the appropriate skill levels and motivation, to complete tasks within the estimated timeframe and budget. Suppose the estimate is not achieving project objectives. In that case, ensure that the level of effort is not changed unilaterally. Project managers can first bring in more resources and rearrange tasks. Then, as a last resort, go back to the team to negotiate changes to effort and its impact on project success.

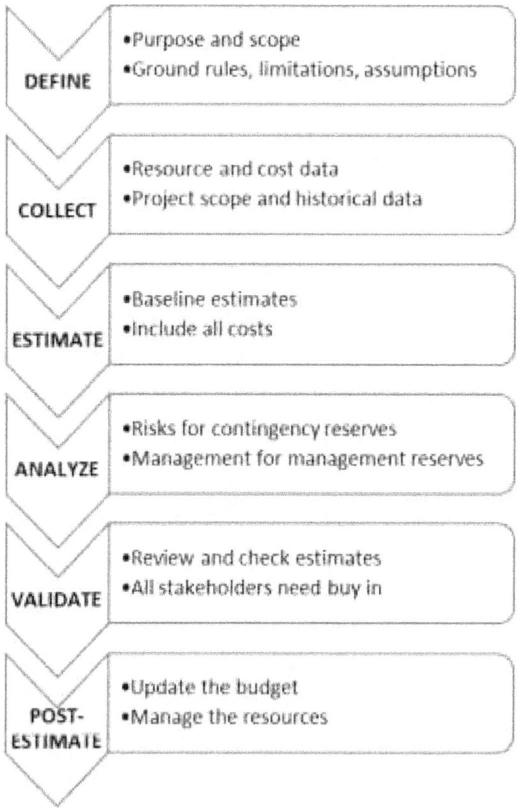

Figure 1: An Estimation Framework

Repeat the process as more project details become known. Conduct lessons learned to improve future iterations.

Common Estimating Mistakes

Many errors can occur when estimating. Some of the most common causes of these mistakes include:

Planning Fallacy: One of hundreds of identified cognitive biases, it is the tendency for people to underestimate the time, resources, and costs required to complete a project. This is because they tend to focus on best-case outcomes. Conversely, they overestimate how much others will take to complete the work. Misjudging estimates leads to unrealistic timelines and budgets.

Cone of Uncertainty: The Cone of Uncertainty is a concept that describes how estimates are less accurate in the early days of a project, when less information is available. As more details become clear, the estimates become more certain. It is a foundational concept for understanding why planning fallacy and incomplete requirements lead to schedule risk. This also means that early planning and estimates should be treated as rough forecasts rather than commitments.

Ignoring Small but Significant Tasks: Overlooking minor tasks can add up, straining schedules and budgets.

Failing to Include All Work: Missing tasks can also add up. Having a clear scope of work and a well-structured WBS will help ensure estimates are as complete and accurate as possible.

Overlooking Inflation, Market Fluctuations, and Other External Forces: Failing to account for changing economic conditions, especially for projects lasting many years, can render estimates inaccurate. Similarly, neglecting to include all local taxes and fees on resources can set a budget back right from the start.

Failing to Involve the Right Stakeholders: Excluding key stakeholders can lead to incomplete or biased estimates.

Agile Estimates

Estimating in agile projects differs substantially from traditional estimating. Rather than determining specific times, agile estimation considers factors such as complexity, difficulty, and risk and compares stories to one another. There is also an underlying assumption and limitation that the development team can maintain a constant velocity, the amount of work they can accomplish in an iteration or sprint. As a result, projects that require accurate estimates are unlikely to use agile estimating techniques.

The simplest form of agile estimation is T-Shirt Sizing. Each story is rated as XS (extra-small), S (small), M (medium), L (large), or XL (extra-large). XS is generally used for minimal tasks, such as correcting a spelling mistake. XL indicates that the story is an epic (a large story) that should be decomposed into stories that fit within a single iteration or sprint. After discussing each story's relative complexity, difficulty, and risk, the team assigns the size.

A drawback of larger projects is that many stories fall into the same size category, making them difficult to compare. Just as shirts made by different designers may vary in size, estimates of user story size will vary (Cohn 2013).

Another form of agile estimating that addresses some of the shortcomings of T-Shirt Sizing is the game, Planning Poker. Poker Planning has more discussion and divides the stories into more categories. These numeric categories are story points. Story points will help determine how the work progresses and how many stories will be completed in an iteration.

With Planning Poker, each team member gets a deck of numbered cards. The numbers are usually Fibonacci numbers with some modification:

0, 1, 2, 3, 5, 8, 13, 20, 40, 100, and ? (unsure)

The larger the number, the greater the complexity, difficulty, and risk associated with the story. Correcting a simple typing mistake in some text might be 0. Developing a simple logon screen might be 1. Securely storing a password with unbreakable encryption might be 8. An epic, which typically requires further breakdown, is usually assigned a score of 100. More significant numbers, such as 20 and 40, might be used for more complex, challenging, and risky features.

During planning poker, the requirements owner reads and describes a story. Each team member then selects a card to represent their estimate, after which everyone simultaneously reveals their selections. Participants with high or low ratings have the opportunity to explain their choices, after which the participants estimate again. Finally, the game continues until the team reaches consensus on each story or epic (Mountain Goat Software, 2020).

Agile projects have issues with time and cost estimates. How, for example, is a large t-shirt size or two story points translated to time, and how is the timeline of the project known upfront? Furthermore, if a project continually introduces new requirements, the timeline may continue to lengthen. An organization that requires upfront time estimates will not tolerate a budget based on agile estimates.

Mitre (2022) suggests, "Estimating [schedules] in an Agile environment requires a more iterative, integrated, and collaborative approach than in traditional programs. [...] [Schedule] estimation on an Agile program is a team-based activity. [...] Ongoing collaboration among the users, development team, systems engineers, [...]

estimators, and other stakeholders is critical to ensure agreement on requirements prioritization in the product backlog and to gain a thorough understanding of the amount of effort required for each release. It also enables an integrated assessment of the operational and programmatic risks, technical performance, cost drivers, affordability, and schedules."

Hybrid Projects

Hybrid projects combine predictive and agile approaches, requiring estimation methods that support upfront planning and adaptive delivery. In hybrid environments, the project manager must reconcile cost-based estimates with relative sizing and team-based forecasts.

Hybrid estimation typically begins with a top-down predictive estimate to establish a high-level timeline, budget, and resource plan. This provides early information executives need to make funding, staffing, and governance decisions. As the project progresses and agile teams refine backlogs, bottom-up agile estimates (e.g., story points, team velocity, or cycle time) replace or refine the initial predictive assumptions.

Translating agile estimates into cost-based units is a significant challenge. Story points do not directly translate into currency; however, once a team has established a stable velocity, the project manager can forecast the number of iterations required to complete backlog items in groups. These iteration-based forecasts can then be integrated into a predictive master schedule.

Hybrid estimation works best when:

- Predictive components involve well-defined deliverables and dependencies.
- Agile components involve evolving requirements or high-uncertainty work.
- The project manager maintains a single master budget schedule that reflects both fixed-date milestones and iterative delivery cycles.

The goal is not to force agile work into a predictive structure, but to create a realistic budget that accounts for each method.

Basis of Estimate

A Basis of Estimate (BoE) is a document that outlines the process for preparing an estimate. Larger, more complex projects may develop a separate document rather than include this information in a single Financial Management Plan document. The topics may include the logic and methodology used for the estimate. For example, if risks are factored in for estimates, this would be covered in the BoE.

There is no universal definition for a BoE document. The BoE most commonly contains the following:

- The work breakdown structure of the project
- Technical activities and their estimates, including sources of data, to meet the requirements of the project
- Any constraints, limitations, risks, and extra activities that need to be done to mitigate risks
- A summary of the estimates
- Known risks and uncertainties of the estimates

- Anything else that needs to be factored in (e.g., ramping up and rolling off staff as the project moves forward, operational costs of resources)

The importance of the BoE is that it not only accounts for the time and costs of individual elements but also considers other factors that may affect them. As a result, this will be closer to actual time and expenses than to any planned time and costs that do not account for other factors. A BoE also makes the estimation process transparent and traceable.

Chapter Summary

This chapter explores the essential concepts, methods, and challenges involved in estimating project duration and effort. It begins by comparing elapsed time (duration) with actual work time (effort), emphasizing the importance of both for accurate scheduling. The chapter also introduces several detailed estimation techniques, including parametric, analogous, and three-point estimates.

A section on PERT explains how weighted averages, standard deviations, and variances combine to produce estimates with confidence ranges. The section also introduces Monte Carlo simulation as a complementary probabilistic method for modeling uncertainty.

Modern estimation methods, such as Function Point Analysis and AI-assisted estimation, are discussed, along with guidance on when and how to apply them. A structured six-step process for improving estimation accuracy is presented, followed by a review of common estimating mistakes, including planning fallacy, the cone of uncertainty, missing tasks, and ignoring external factors.

The chapter concludes with an overview of agile estimation techniques, the challenges of translating story points into time, and the role of hybrid estimation in mixed-method environments. Finally, it explains the purpose and structure of a Basis of Estimate (BoE) document, reinforcing the importance of documenting assumptions, methods, and risks to improve the transparency and traceability of estimates.

- **Formulas**: 3-point estimate, PERT

Knowledge Nuggets

Chapter Template: PERT Estimation Template

Chapter Pro Tip: Despite internet articles to the contrary, PERT and FPA can be valuable for many projects outside software-related industries, not just for scheduling.

PERT estimation was part of a larger system and was designed to focus on schedules. Its benefit is that it provides, mathematically, everything an estimate should include, including a range and a confidence level.

Often, schedules are uncertain, so having three estimation points can help address that. Costs are also uncertain and can be estimated using the same method.

Similarly, FPA was initially designed to measure the repeatable units of software projects (e.g., lines of code, functions, subroutines, and other code packages). However, many projects in other industries have repeatable units. FPA can also be applied to these projects.

Finally, do not fear mixing techniques. For example, US Patent number 7,801,834 B2 (Method and Apparatus for Estimating Tool) describes a system that includes order-of-magnitude and function-point analysis estimates, with calculated ranges. It was designed to estimate software configuration projects with a limited number of potential configurations. Choose the estimating methods that best fit your project needs, regardless of the industry or application they were originally designed for.

CHAPTER 7

Chapter 7: The Basics of Budgets

According to the sixth edition of the PMBOK® Guide, "a project budget includes all the funds authorized to execute the project. The cost baseline is the approved version of the time-phased project budget but excludes management reserves (PMI 2017)."

Unlike corporate balance sheets and income statements, project budgets typically focus on expenses rather than revenues. However, revenue is possible for some industry projects, such as planning. Revenues are typically a part of the sales or product management process. Sales must meet revenue targets established by senior management.

Therefore, there are at least two cases where a project manager may need to estimate and monitor revenues (and other scenarios may be possible):

- Project managers in a dual project and product management role
- Project managers of self-funded projects (i.e., projects where the revenue of the first project phase funds subsequent phases).

What is a Budget?

Let us unpack the PMBOK Guide (Sixth Edition) definition. The budget is the total amount of funds that management authorizes for the project. At the end of planning, the cost baseline is the approved budget. A large, complex project may be over multiple periods (e.g., quarters, months, or years). Still, minor, more straightforward projects may have a single period (e.g., five months), regardless of their overall duration.

Budget responsibility varies depending on organizational size and culture, project complexity, and assigned roles and responsibilities. Therefore, project managers need to be familiar with all aspects of budgeting and treat cost management as one of the most flexible knowledge areas in the PMBOK Guide.

Managers in product development may be required to consider revenue. The revenue budgeting principles are very similar to those for expenses. However, those managing products also need to trace cash flow to defend their product.

For example, one project manager we know was denied funding to improve a product given to all users for free. Tracing cash flow, they found that half of the revenue from another high-margin product would be lost if the "free" product were removed. They successfully secured the necessary funding to improve the product using that argument.

As this definition states, management reserves are excluded. What are they? Management reserves are funds set aside to cover costs arising from unidentified project risks.

Include another type of reserve, contingency reserves, in the budget. Contingency reserves are funds set aside to cover costs arising from identified project risks.

Contingency reserves[7] may be computed based on a rigorous risk management process. Alternatively, many organizations may set aside a percentage of the budget, typically under 25%, for the contingency reserve. We will examine how to compute reserves and other aspects of budget implementation in the remainder of this chapter.

Categorizing Costs

As you may know from the book *Risk Assessment Framework: Successfully Navigating Uncertainty*, we firmly believe that having categories and prompt lists can help with brainstorming. While some budget estimates can be computed, most of the work is ensuring that all costs are included. Therefore, it is critical to consider all the charges, including taxes, fees, and economic conditions. In addition, one or more of these categories may require a budget breakdown.

Here are six ways to view project costs to ensure they are all accounted for and that your monitoring and control efforts are successful.

People, Equipment, and Material Costs. This first category is recognizable as the project management definition of resources. This categorization is excellent for identifying project resources and breaking them into three major categories. Be careful to include all costs, including fees, operating costs, and taxes.

Direct vs. Indirect Costs. Direct costs are those directly attributable to the project. For example, they might include expenses such as

---

[7] The PMBOK Guide Eighth Edition changes the definition slightly, recognizing that contingency reserves may or may not be a part of the budget. We lean toward having it in the budget to be reminded of it.

salaries and training, specialized software or tools needed for the project, and materials such as lumber, nails, and chemicals. Indirect costs are shared costs, such as office leases for a headquarters building or shared copy machines.

Depending on your organization's financial and budget policies and practices, you may need to track some portion of indirect costs. Also, it is important to know how the purchased item is applied and how it relates to the project. For example, do not just assume leases are indirect costs. We have managed projects in which specific work locations had to be leased solely for the project; these were direct costs.

Fixed vs. Variable Costs. Fixed costs are those that remain relatively constant. For example, they might include the cost of a computer or a fixed fee paid. Variable costs vary and are harder to predict. In most cases, these costs are expressed as "per use" or "per hour." Therefore, it will be critical to maintain an accurate schedule to estimate variable costs accurately.

Tangible vs. Intangible Costs. Tangible costs are costs of items that we can see, touch, or feel. Most project resources will fall into this category. Intangible costs are for non-physical resources, and are also more challenging to estimate. These costs might include project waste (e.g., wasted time, inefficient work, rework).

Intangible costs are subjective values placed on circumstances or events and may include factors such as reputation or happiness. For example, unhappy project team members may not work efficiently, wasting more time. This wasted time may directly affect tangible costs, such as equipment downtime. Therefore, finding ways to keep team members happy will keep project costs down.

Deciding whether an item is tangible or intangible often requires the assistance of a corporate accounting professional. For example, in both the US and the UK, there are circumstances in which software (generally considered intangible) may be treated as tangible.

Operational Costs. Some equipment may incur operating costs. Costs could include fuel, electricity, maintenance, other energy sources, and more. As you review your budget, include all operating costs for equipment and materials.

Sunk Costs. Sunk costs are those costs that have already been expended. These are also actual costs paid each period. While it can be emotionally tricky, do not let sunk costs influence important project decisions. For example, suppose you spend $1m only to find there is no way to complete the project successfully. In that case, the project should likely be canceled. Instead, find a way to make productive use of work already completed. Do not let that $1m already spent keep you from making the right decision.

Taxation

Taxes are compulsory financial charges imposed by governments on individuals or businesses. Taxes can affect both revenue and expenses.

Taxes on procurements are often overlooked when planning project budgets. Taxes may be known by various names, such as Value Added Tax (VAT), Goods and Services Tax (GST), or sales tax. They are often a percentage above the price of the item or service purchased. For example, if a machine costs $100,000, there may be an additional 7.5% VAT, bringing the total to $ 107,500. Therefore, project managers need to account for applicable taxes in their financial planning and management.

Certain taxes can be claimed back from the government, adding complexity. For example, if the 7.5% VAT paid on the machine is claimable, it should be reflected in the project accounts. The company's accountant is best positioned to explain which procurements are taxable and which are eligible for a refund. Take care to identify them so you can manage project finances correctly.

Capital Budgeting, Depreciation, and Amortization

Capital budgeting evaluates the returns from projects or other major purchases of plants and equipment, expensive licenses, or other significant assets. These purchases are paid for immediately in cash or purchased with a loan. Still, the purchasing organization may recognize the asset's cost over time.

Representing the expense over time encourages investment. The encouragement happens through a compromise. First, the cost impact on the company's balance sheet is reduced, providing a more favorable picture. Second, the period is determined by "useful life," an accounting concept.

Accountants determine the useful life, which is usually shorter than an asset's actual operating time. Computers, for example, are often written off over three to five years, but can often be used in production for many years beyond their useful life. Once they are written off (i.e., all the expenses have been recognized), companies still have an operating asset. Therefore, they can invest in other needs, establishing a cycle of upgrades to plants and equipment that enable continuous improvement to the business's operations.

Expenses are usually recognized over time using a process known as depreciation. Depreciation determines how much of the cost should be recognized each year. It is based on the loss of value due to wear and tear or obsolescence. Project managers may need to track depreciation in project budgets or contribute to corporate financial statements (e.g., the profit and loss (P&L) statement and the balance sheet).

Do not approach complex capital budgeting and depreciation topics without first discussing them with the finance or accounting department. In addition, accountants and tax agencies recognize more than two dozen depreciation methods. We will examine two, as illustrated in the following table.

Assumptions: 4-year useful life, no salvage value	Year 0	Year 1	Year 2	Year 3	Year 4
Balance Sheet: crane	$500,000	$ 375,000	$250,000	$125,000	$0
P&L or Project Budget: straight line	$0	$ 125,000	$125,000	$125,000	$125,000
Balance Sheet: Software License	$500,000	$ 300,000	$150,000	$50,000	$0
P&L or Project Budget: sum of the years	$0	$ 200,000	$150,000	$100,000	$50,000

Table 2: Sample Depreciation[8]

In straight-line depreciation, subtract any salvage value[9] from the purchase price. Divide the remaining quantity by the years of useful life. Then, each year, the same amount of the expense is reported on the profit and loss statement (in the crane case, one-fourth of the $500,000 cost, with no salvage value). We see the $500,000 asset on the balance sheet in the crane's year of purchase. In

[8] Year 0 represents a point in time when the asset is acquired.

[9] The salvage value is the value we can sell or trade an asset for when disposing of it, normally at the end of its useful life.

subsequent years, the asset's value decreases by $125,000 due to straight-line depreciation.

$$Annual\ salvage\ value = \frac{purchase\ price - salvage\ value}{years\ of\ useful\ life}$$

Equation 10: Straight-line Depreciation

The software license illustrates a "sum of the years" technique. In this case, a fraction of the expense, less the salvage value, is represented on the profit and loss statement each year. First, determine the denominator of the fractions by adding the years (i.e., 4 + 3 + 2 + 1 = 10). The years, in reverse order, become the numerators. So for the first year, 4/10, or 40%, of the expense is reflected on the P&L statement. After that, 30%, 20%, and 10% are applied in subsequent years until the asset is fully depreciated (Goodpasture 2004).

Amortization records the payoff of a loan used for capital purchases or the write-down of an intangible asset (i.e., goodwill). When used for assets, amortization is approximately equivalent to depreciation. We will examine project loans in more detail in the chapter "Project Finance."

Currency Conversions

International business usually involves multiple currencies. If there are overseas suppliers, you can pay in their currency. However, avoid this unless there is an excellent reason. Overseas suppliers should be asked to submit their bids and invoices in your currency, with the banks handling exchange rates.

In some cases, you may want to choose a third country's currency to conduct your business. For example, suppose you are in Indonesia, and your supplier is in South Africa. In that case, you may choose the US dollar as the common currency for all your budgeting and invoicing.

If you need to pay invoices in multiple currencies, you should request exchange rates from the finance department. However, your budget should be in one currency. Global companies set internal currency exchange rates for budgeting (but not for actual payments, which are processed at the bank's exchange rates). However, if there is a significant fluctuation in currency exchange rates, the finance department may revise the internal exchange rates. If this happens, budgets need to be adjusted. The project manager should track these changes to manage costs.

Budget Reserve Planning

To start the reserve planning process, a completed risk analysis is required.[10] First, estimate the financial impact for each risk, then compute the estimated monetary value (EMV). The EMV is the product of the likelihood and the impact in dollars or your local currency. Also, consider that risks can have both positive and negative consequences.

While it may have some shortcomings, one of the simplest ways to compute budget contingency reserves is:

---

[10] For details on how to complete a risk analysis, see our companion publication, *Risk Assessment Framework: Successfully Navigating Uncertainty*.

$$CR = \sum_{1}^{n} EMV$$

where:

CR = Contingency Reserve
EMV = Estimated Monetary Value
n = Number of Risks

Equation 11: Contingency Reserve Calculation

Look at the hard-dollar impact (actual costs) and any soft-dollar impact (costs that are difficult to estimate, such as those generated by goodwill or a reputation change). Perhaps a large amount of money is not at stake. Still, the organization's credibility is at risk, which could reduce sales by a large but difficult-to-estimate amount. Therefore, do not add soft-dollar impacts to the reserve; list them separately to support the reserve.

It may not be unusual for some organizations to assign a fixed percentage (typically 5-15%) of the initiative budget for contingency reserves. However, good project managers will perform the actual computations and review them to avoid surprises later in the initiative.

Contingency reserve differs from management reserve. Management reserve is not a part of the budget. Instead, it is the amount that management is willing to set aside for the unidentified risks. The estimate is usually determined using a top-down approach, such as a rule of thumb or simply what the budget allows. Management may elect not to share the management reserve and use it at their discretion.

Budgets and Rolling Wave Planning

Rolling wave planning is an incremental approach to project planning. With rolling wave planning, near-term work is planned in detail, while future work is only scheduled at a high level. As time passes, the plan continues to elaborate on near-term work further.

Rolling wave planning is ideal for long-term, complex projects, such as constructing an intranational, international, or transnational highway network. However, it can be used whenever there is uncertainty in a project's key components, such as the schedule and budget. It is also similar to how Scrum operates for Agile projects, where each iteration determines costs and schedules.

Being successful with budgeting requires several things. First, robust program management must be in place to ensure that all components and projects operate and spend as effectively as possible. Second, this form of planning usually works best in environments where budget is not a significant concern or where funding intervals are regular. Regular intervals enable funders and projects to have reconciliation periods (Mill 2020).

Agile and hybrid projects with many unknowns often require rolling-wave planning. On the other hand, rolling-wave planning is usually unnecessary for predictive projects. The important lesson is that if a project is short or requires budget accuracy, rolling wave planning is not recommended. Furthermore, Agile is not recommended in these circumstances because it is akin to rolling-wave planning.

Chapter Summary

Chapter 7 explains the fundamentals of project budgets. Project budgets focus primarily on expenses, though some project managers, especially those in product-related roles, may also need to estimate and track revenue.

The chapter clarifies the difference between the budget and the cost baseline, and distinguishes contingency reserves (for identified risks) from management reserves (for unknown risks), noting that management reserves are excluded from the budget.

A major section covers cost categorization, emphasizing that complete budgets require identifying all cost types: people, equipment, materials, direct vs. indirect, fixed vs. variable, tangible vs. intangible, operational costs, and sunk costs. The text warns against letting sunk costs influence decisions, reminding readers that "the project should likely be canceled" if it cannot succeed, regardless of the money already spent.

Practical budgeting considerations such as taxation, capital budgeting and depreciation, currency conversions, and reserve planning using Estimated Monetary Value (EMV) are also highlighted. The importance of including taxes, understanding depreciation methods, and keeping budgets in a single currency, even when vendors operate internationally, is stressed.

Finally, the chapter introduces rolling wave planning, an incremental approach useful for long, complex, or uncertain projects. While effective in Agile and hybrid environments, it is not recommended for short projects or those requiring high budget accuracy.

- **Formulas**: Contingency reserve calculation and depreciation

Knowledge Nuggets

Chapter Template: Depreciation Calculation Template

Chapter Pro Tip: Always seek management guidance and make friends with your cost accountant.

As we point out throughout this text, managing project costs requires flexibility. Flexibility is required because project finances must integrate with the larger organization's financial systems. Therefore, finance and accounting professionals in a finance department typically seek practices that align with their own needs and meet those of their executive stakeholders.

Some specific concerns to watch out for include, but are not limited to:

- Estimation requirements and techniques
- Budget requirements and formats
    - Mixed currencies and currency conversions
    - Reserves
    - Handling of indirect costs
    - Impacts of taxation and inflation
- Regulatory requirements
- Capital investment and expenditure requirements

To learn more about these practices, consult with your manager or Project Management Office. Consulting with them will save time and help you develop accurate estimates and budgets in the most appropriate format, ensuring you meet all requirements the first time.

Cost accountants and other financial professionals can also be invaluable resources when learning about the organization, typical costs, and other financial data. Here are just three instances of how projects benefit from financial professionals:

- Salary estimates were needed to complete a budget, but the project manager did not have access to that data. Instead, a cost accountant provided anonymous company data on average salaries for various positions and skill levels, enabling the budget to be completed.
- A project was turned down because management did not want to invest in a free product. In addition, the project manager suspected that the free product accounted for a large share of revenue but had no idea by how much. Much to their surprise, a cost accountant informed them that the revenue generated exceeded half of the company's total revenue. The project manager presented this information to management and the risk to revenue if the project is not moved forward. The project received approval.
- A project manager with multiple projects for finance managers was asked to implement a simplified version of Earned Value Management (EVM) for status reports. The finance department told the project manager that bills providing actual costs were prepared for these finance managers on Friday mornings. The data could be made available to the project manager. This data enabled the project manager to implement a simplified EVM and meet the Friday status-report requirement.

CHAPTER 8

Chapter 8: Budget Presentation

Having covered all the information necessary to identify and calculate the components of a budget, let us now look at the different ways to present it. However, before we do that, just one more planning detail.

Suppose we are managing a waterfall or predictive project. A best practice is to associate estimates with a Work Breakdown Structure (WBS). Use a WBS Dictionary to record cost estimates for their work packages. If the project is agile, the closest analogy is the Product Backlog. At this point, assemble the estimates into the budget for presentation.

The Importance of Including All Costs

Assembling the estimates into a presentable format allows one to check that all costs are included. A second look is critical, as the expectation is that the final budget will be within 5-10% of the actual budget.

Some everyday costs to forget include sales taxes, fees, and equipment operating costs. In some areas, sales taxes can be as high as 11%. Should taxable materials be a large portion of the overall budget, say 50%, you will have already used up your 5% cushion.

For longer-term, human-resource-intensive projects, economic conditions may also be significant. For example, if the workforce receives an 8% year-over-year salary increase, the cushion will be exceeded.

General Budget Best Practices

Perhaps an essential practice is always to follow organizational financial and project management policies and templates, where available. Conforming to standards will ensure your project is reviewed and compared quickly with other projects.

The basic rules for dealing with numbers in budgets are:

- Use a single, preferred currency,
- Use only whole numbers appropriately rounded,
- Enclose negative numbers in parentheses and use a red font if available (as opposed to using the minus sign),
- Only use the currency symbol for the top and bottom items in a column or group of items in a column,
- Numbers greater than a thousand should include commas (or periods, depending on your locale) to separate thousands (the use of "accounting" format with no decimal places in spreadsheet software will address this requirement), and
- Writing (1 million) or (1,000 thousand) is far clearer than -1,000,022.53

- Single underline subtotals, double underline grand totals

Be sure to document all assumptions so that the reader can easily determine how various estimates were derived.

If you need to address revenues and costs, group all revenues first. Then, the costs will form a second group. Finally, each group should end with a total, and a net total, the expenses subtracted from the revenues, should be placed as a final item.

For a first draft, resist the urge to "tune" the numbers or solve problems by changing numbers, even with assumptions. Many decisions are best with team input; project managers should not make them unilaterally. Instead, let the first draft "speak for itself" as you present it to various stakeholders for review and have appropriate problem-solving and decision-making meetings.

WBS-Based Budgets

A budget is easiest to format using the Work Breakdown Structure (WBS). A simple two-column presentation is possible, with the WBS deliverables on the right and the budgeted costs on the left. In addition to getting the total cost, rolling up the levels in the WBS hierarchy provides additional subtotals. Be sure to add an item for contingency reserves near the bottom.

Once the budget is complete, some organizations may add accounts to the WBS work packages. These will help track costs throughout the project and provide valuable financial information to management.

Budget for Project Team Breakfast				
WBS Level	WBS	Cost	Totals	Notes
Level 2	Bacon & Eggs	$ 60		8 dozen eggs, 4 1-lb packages bacon
Level 2	Drinks		$ 49	Drinks Total
Level 3	Orange Juice	28		4 gallons
Level 3	Tea	6		100 tea bags
Level 3	Coffee	15		30 oz medium roast coffee
Level 2	Toast	24		6 loaves
Contingency		$ 27		Assume 20% of budget
Level 2 Total			133	
Level 3 Total			49	
Project Total			$ 160	

Figure 2: Sample WBS-based Budget

Activity-Based Budgets

While a WBS-based budget is deliverable-based, an activity-based budget is project-activity-based. Therefore, if a WBS with estimates exists, the first step is to develop a high-level schedule (if a schedule has not already been created) and allocate costs to activities. This strategy provides an additional opportunity to ensure that all costs are considered. The team can discuss work and costs, which may help identify unnecessary work, previously hidden costs, work bottlenecks, and opportunities for efficiency.

As with the WBS-based budget, a simple two-column presentation is possible, with activities on the left, budgeted costs on the right, and contingency reserves at the bottom. In addition to getting the total cost, rolling up the levels in the WBS hierarchy may provide additional activity subtotals.

Budget for Project Team Breakfast				
Activity		Cost	Totals	Notes
Cooking			$ 84	
	Bacon & Eggs	$ 60		8 dozen eggs, 4 1-lb packages bacon
	Toast	24		6 loaves
Serving			49	
	Orange Juice	28		4 gallons
	Tea	6		100 tea bags
	Coffee	15		30 oz medium roast coffee
Contingency			$ 27	Assume 20% of budget
Project Total			$ 160	

Figure 3: Sample Activity-based Budget

Other Presentations and Time-Phased Budgets

Many organizations have evolved budget requirements and templates to meet their own accounting needs. For example, they may be similar to WBS-based, activity-based, or resource-based approaches. Rather than reinventing the wheel, it is best to check with your manager, the finance department, or the PMO before finalizing a template.

As the definition of a budget states, a budget is time-based. Simple, short projects may have a single period based on their duration. More complex, longer projects may need a budget breakdown by month, quarter, year, or business period. Time-based budgets may require contingency reserves spread over the project's life or aligned with the final period.

Project Management Symposium Budget

	Units	*Cost per Unit*	*Amount*	*Year 2*	*Notes*
Revenues					
Registrations	275	225	$61,875	$61,875	
Exhibition Hall Fees	35	50	1,750	1,750	35 vendors pay $50 per table
Platinum Sponsor	1	1,000	1,000	1,000	
Gold Sponsor	2	500	1,000	1,000	
Silver Sponsor	5	250	1,250	1,250	
Bronze Sponsor	8	50	400	400	
Pearl Sponsor	10	20	200	200	
Total Revenues			$67,475	$67,475	
Expenses					
Venue	1	1,000	$4,000	$4,120	
Hotel Rooms	10	199	7,960	8,199	4 nights for 10
Lighting Rental	1	450	1,800	1,854	for 4 days
Internet Access	1	200	800	824	for 4 days
Insurance	1	5,000	5,000	5,150	
Printing	400	25	9,800	10,094	
Printing Fee	1	75	75	77	
Reception	325	20	26,000	26,780	
Exhibition Hall	1	1,500	6,000	6,180	
Advertising	1	600	600	618	one time cost
Total Expenses			$62,035	$63,896	
Gross Profit			$5,440	$3,579	

Figure 4: Sample Time-Phased Budget with Alternative Format

Chapter Summary

Chapter 8 explains how to assemble and present a project budget once all estimates have been developed. It begins by reinforcing that predictive projects should tie estimates to the Work Breakdown Structure (WBS), while Agile projects rely on the Product Backlog. Once estimates are organized, they are compiled into a presentable budget.

A key reminder is to include all costs, since missing items, such as taxes, fees, or equipment operating costs, can quickly erode the expected 5–10% budget accuracy range. A review is critical, especially for long-term or labor-intensive projects where economic conditions may shift.

The chapter outlines general budgeting best practices, including using a single currency, rounding to whole numbers, formatting negative numbers in parentheses, documenting assumptions, and grouping revenues before costs when both appear. It also advises letting the first draft "speak for itself" before making adjustments, ensuring decisions are made collaboratively rather than unilaterally.

Three major budget presentation formats are described:

- WBS-based budgets, which align costs with deliverables and allow subtotals to roll up through the hierarchy.
- Activity-based budgets, which align costs with scheduled activities and help reveal hidden work, bottlenecks, or unnecessary tasks.
- Time-phased budgets, which break costs into periods (months, quarters, years) to reflect how funds will be spent over time.

Organizations may have their own templates, so project managers should confirm requirements before finalizing the presentation.

Knowledge Nuggets

Chapter Template: Budget Presentation Template

Chapter Pro Tip: Resist the temptation to fix budget issues by immediately raising prices or slashing costs.

When creating budgets, it is not unusual to encounter issues. The issues may range from higher-than-expected costs to lower-than-expected revenues. However, project managers are problem solvers and need to approach budget issues correctly.

I have seen many project managers who want to raise prices immediately to increase revenue or slash costs to meet cost targets. This approach will not yield the best results. Increased prices may reduce sales, and slashed expenses may reduce quality or scope, creating unintended consequences. Instead, put together a first draft budget without changing the team's estimates. Then take it back to the team and highlight the key issues that require solutions.

Facilitate the team's identification of multiple potential solutions for each issue. Aim for three to five, and remember that postponing a decision or doing nothing is an implicit choice. Then, list the pros and cons for each. Finally, reach a consensus on the best solution. Now would be an excellent time to engage key stakeholders. Share the ideas with them and get their feedback. Then make a decision and create another draft budget.

A careful, thoughtful approach to problem-solving and decision-making will lead to success. The success of the decision depends on:

- The diversity and quality of information and data available,
- The quality of the process followed, and
- The implementation of the decision.

CHAPTER **9**

CHAPTER 9: PROJECT FINANCING

Project financing concerns how project costs will be covered and paid. Depending on the industry you work in, a project manager's involvement in financing projects may come sooner rather than later. As a project manager, you may also need to manage financing costs. This chapter aims not to provide challenging financial calculations or make you a project financing expert but to expose you to essential principles, concepts, and terms.

Consistent with one of the overarching themes of project cost management, project managers will need to rely on organizational financial experts from the finance department, the Project Management Office (PMO), or their manager for guidance on corporate policies, procedures, tools, and templates. Their advice is crucial for new project managers or those with first-time financial responsibilities on projects. In addition, as noted earlier, a cost accountant will help fill any gaps in cost and local practice information.

How are Projects Funded?

One way to finance projects is self-financing. There are three significant ways projects can be self-financed:

- Corporate income from operations is immediately spent on projects. This income may often be derived from agile projects that regularly deliver monetizable benefits.
- Projects may also be treated as capital expenses. Businesses retain prior-year earnings, and their treasury operations reinvest them in the business. Capital expenses may be allocated to the acquisition, upgrade, or maintenance of any owned property, buildings, or significant equipment.
- Projects may be cross-subsidized by other projects or programs in the portfolio. Cross-subsidies are common in the oil industry, where successful wells pay for unsuccessful ones and generate profits.

As an alternative, organizations may take out loans to fund projects. However, projects financed with loans can be problematic if they fail. Not only must the principal be repaid, but interest will also be due. In addition, some substantial projects are often funded with unsecured loans or loans secured by future revenue streams. If these projects fail, the lender is also impacted and not repaid.

Project financing can impose significant pressures on the organization, the project, and the project manager. The funding must typically:

- Be in place to start the project
- Consider that lenders are now stakeholders
- Not impact project benefits and value
- Consider cost control and cash flows

Interest payments under project financing may add additional budget pressure, so explore financing options early. The time may be as soon as project feasibility is investigated or as initial concerns about adding the project to the portfolio occur. In general, projects may be financed by conventional or unconventional means, and we will examine these next.

Project Structures

Three unique project structures can affect financing and other aspects of cost management. While these are more common in the public sector, some non-public-sector projects have adopted them as well. The models are included here for completeness and must be considered in financing.

Build, Operate, and Own (BOO). An interesting project type is BOO, where an organization builds, owns, and operates an entity on behalf of another party. Payments are received only based on the project's primary deliverable income.

These projects are common in the public sector, particularly in public-private partnerships (PPPs). Typically, a government would ask a private-sector organization to build and operate a facility, such as an airport, and share in the airport's revenue. BOO projects are attractive to governments because they do not require public funds. They are also appealing to private organizations that adopt them, as they are often eligible for tax concessions.

Recently, BOO projects have become common in private organizations, especially in the telecom and hospitality sectors. In this case, one organization builds, owns, and operates a business under another company's brand.

Revenue from BOO projects begins to be generated once the project is operational. As a result, there is always a sense of urgency to complete BOO projects more quickly. Also, there is a tendency to be optimistic when planning. Project managers need to balance business needs (e.g., generating revenue as early as possible) and project needs (e.g., ensuring products meet safety requirements).

Build, Operate, and Transfer (BOT). BOT projects are very similar to BOO projects with one key difference. The organization that builds and operates the project's outcome must transfer it to the other entity within a specific period. For example, a government may ask a private organization to build an airport, operate it for 10 years, receive revenue from it, and then transfer ownership to the government.

This difference creates an even greater sense of urgency and more stringent revenue planning. Both BOO and BOT projects require very stringent revenue planning to determine whether the expected project benefits are realized and whether the funding organization considers the project profitable. These structures will indirectly affect the project manager. The project manager often reacts by cutting funding when the project is delayed. This reaction, unfortunately, leads to a spiraling impact.

Build, Lease, and Transfer (BLT). One way to mitigate the financial risk of BOO and BOT projects is the BLT approach. With this approach, the public-sector partner (or the party that contracted out the project) provides a fixed amount of money to the party that built the project, as a lease. The lease removes the private sector partner's risks. In addition, it reduces pressure on the project manager because the income would be predictable.

Conventional Financing

There are two primary types of conventional financing – equity and debt. Investors providing this type of financing include banks, investment firms, venture capitalists, shareholders, and suppliers.

Some projects may be financed through equity or ownership interests. Investors receive dividends or capital gains in proportion to their investment. Venture capital firms often fund technology projects and innovative products in exchange for a stake in the company that undertakes the project. TV shows such as Shark Tank and Dragon's Den have removed some of the mystery of how this type of financing works.

The contractors may fund some projects in exchange for equity. For example, approximately 20% of the financing for the Eurotunnel, or "Chunnel," was provided through equity grants to contractors and private investors.

Equity investments can be riskier for investors. First, their distributions can occur only after all interest and loan repayments have been made. For some projects, this can take many years. In addition, there are only returns if the project is successful. Should the project fail, the entire investment may be lost. As a result, investors who provide cash in exchange for equity typically demand higher returns than investors in projects.

Debt is a conventional form of project financing, typically in the form of loans or bonds. Debt involves periodic repayment of the loan, with interest, according to agreed-upon schedules. Debt may be secured by cash or valuable assets, such as a home used as collateral for a mortgage. Debt may also be unsecured; however, there is a higher risk. For example, if the project fails, repayment of the lender or bondholder may not be possible.

Loans and bonds are senior debt. With senior debt, the borrower must pay it off before other debt. Senior debt holders can also make the first claims on an organization's assets if a project fails. In addition, any secured debt must be repaid under all circumstances. If repayment is not possible, the lenders will take possession of the cash or assets offered as security. Since unsecured debt carries a higher risk, those providing unsecured debt financing often seek higher returns on their investment.

When a project fails or fails to deliver planned benefits, an organization may be unable to pay its debts. The Eurotunnel, which was approximately 80% debt-financed, is one example: its early revenues were insufficient to repay the debt. In this case, lenders may renegotiate to become equity holders. As a result, Eurotunnel's equity holders received a share of future revenues, which helped offset some losses.

Another source of debt financing is loans from equity holders, which are also repaid at predetermined rates. This type of debt is mezzanine debt. Mezzanine debt can be repaid only after all senior debt has been repaid. Since mezzanine debt typically carries more risk, it is priced for higher interest rates.

Unconventional Financing

Unlike conventional financing, there are many different means of unconventional financing. New ideas and new combinations of old ideas seem to spring up regularly. Let us look at some of the most common methods for unconventional funding:

Finance lease: A finance lease transfers the risks and rewards of ownership to the lessee. The lessor acquires the asset and provides it to the lessee for a fixed periodic payment. Project cash is freed by acquiring an asset for small, fixed payments. Given the temporary nature of projects, it often makes sense to lease any required workspace. The project may be long-term, or the facility may be used for operations later.

Finance leasing is also typically used when a project needs industrial vehicles or equipment. When the project completes, the asset may be put into operation under a new lease, or either party may sell it to pay off the remaining costs owed to the lessor.

Countertrade: A countertrade occurs when goods or services are accepted as payment. The recipient needs to sell the goods or use the services received to raise funds for the project. Countertrade is most common among startups and international projects involving economically developing countries. Countertrade is beneficial when there is insufficient cash to finance a project and a commodity is in surplus.

When using countertrade, it is essential to monitor cash flow. However, cash is still necessary for operations, so too many countertrades can be harmful. There are six different types of countertrade transactions:

- **Barter**: Purchased goods are paid for with other goods. Barter is a less popular form of countertrade. It may not be simple to market and sell the goods received instead of payment, or to agree on an acceptable exchange rate for them.
- **Compensation**: The goods offered in payment are transferred to a third party. The third party may either be a consumer or a seller of these goods. For example, this trade may be used to pay off another debt, fund operations, or sell the goods, with the profits split among the parties.

- **Buyback**: This is the most popular form of countertrade. In exchange for providing an asset, such as a factory, needed for an expansion project, the provider agrees to purchase or accept a specified amount of the factory's output as compensation for establishing it. Such agreements are usually long-term and exceed the required payment.
- **Counterpurchase**: This is a more complex but widespread form of countertrade. A counterpurchase is a type of countertrade involving a two-part agreement. In addition to accepting goods and services as payment, a second agreement is executed to purchase unrelated goods and services as a condition of the exchange. In some cases, an exchange may be like both a countertrade and a counterpurchase (Investopedia 2026).
- **Switch trading**: A company sells its obligation to another to purchase goods in a country.
- **Offset**: This is an agreement where one country purchases from another, subject to the project buyer purchasing raw materials and goods from the seller or agreeing to manufacture the product in the buyer's country (Wikipedia 2020).

International aid funding: The transfer of cash, goods, or services from one country to another, also known as foreign aid, can fund projects. While some transactions are processed through international financial institutions, such as the World Bank, assistance may also come directly from another country. For example, China's Belt and Road Initiative (BRI) invests in ports, buildings, airports, bridges, and other infrastructure projects across more than 70 countries (CFR 2020).

Crowdfunding: This method allows many individuals to make small contributions to a project's funding, sometimes in exchange for perks. Platforms such as Kickstarter take a portion of the funds as payment for brokering donations and projects.

Microfunding: Microfunding, also known as microlending, is the practice of lending small amounts of money to businesses without using a bank. Services or mentoring are often provided, and the loans are interest-only and fee-free.

The Cost of Financing

Debt and equity financing, as well as many unconventional funding sources, entail additional costs to consider (e.g., interest payments). Consider these costs as they may significantly impact the financing decision. In addition, they may be beyond the project manager's expertise, so be sure to consult finance professionals.

The cost of debt financing may consist of fees and interest rates. The availability of funds, security deposits, economic conditions, borrower credit rating, and repayment timing may affect these fees and rates. Credit card debt is typically the highest unless paid off within the allotted time. Note that the cost of debt financing is generally paid from taxed income.

On the other hand, equity financing is typically paid from untaxed income. The cost of equity is the dividends paid to equity holders plus an estimate of the equity's growth rate. Equity often involves giving up some control over the project or organization. Furthermore, equity and bond financing may entail additional costs, including payments to accountants, advisors, attorneys, and market makers.

A combination of debt and equity may finance many large projects. In this case, the cost of capital is the ratio of equity times the cost of equity plus the ratio of debt times the cost of debt (Venkataraman & Pinto 2008).

$$\text{Cost of capital} = \text{Ratio of equity} * \text{Cost of equity} + \text{Ratio of debt} * \text{Cost of debt}$$

Equation 12: Calculating the Cost of Capital

Chapter Summary

Chapter 9 introduces the fundamentals of project financing: how projects are funded, how financing structures work, and how financing decisions affect project managers. The chapter emphasizes that project managers are not expected to be financial experts, and they must rely on organizational financial experts for guidance on corporate policies, procedures, tools, and templates.

Projects may be funded through self-financing (e.g., operational income) or through loans, which add repayment and interest burdens if the project underperforms. Because financing affects cash flow, benefits, and stakeholder expectations, project managers must understand funding constraints early.

The chapter describes three project structures that influence financing:

- **BOO (Build, Operate, Own)** – the builder owns and operates the asset, earning revenue directly.
- **BOT (Build, Operate, Transfer)** – similar to BOO, but ownership eventually transfers to another party.
- **BLT (Build, Lease, Transfer)** – reduces private-sector risk by providing predictable lease payments.

It then outlines conventional financing (equity and debt), explaining that equity investors assume greater risk and expect higher returns. In contrast, debt financing requires scheduled repayment and may be secured or unsecured. The Eurotunnel example illustrates how heavy debt loads can create long-term financial strain.

The chapter also covers unconventional financing, including finance leases, countertrade arrangements (such as barter, buyback, and counterpurchase), international aid, crowdfunding, and microfunding. These methods can support projects when cash is limited or when traditional financing is unavailable.

Finally, the chapter explains the cost of financing, including interest, fees, dividends, and the cost of capital. These costs may significantly impact the financing decision, reinforcing the need for project managers to collaborate closely with finance professionals

- **Formula**: Cost of capital

Knowledge Nuggets

Chapter Pro Tip: Use these six tips to stay out of debt, whether business or personal, projects or organizations.

Review the budget. Carefully review the budget line-by-line. Understanding how you earn and spend is a critical first step in managing debt. Be sure the budget is reasonably accurate, realistic, and up to date. The exercise will yield data to inform your next steps.

Increase revenues. More revenue creates more opportunities to pay off debt. One way to increase revenues is to increase sales. More cash will be available to pay off debt if you can drive more sales. In addition to increasing sales efforts, one way to drive more sales is to offer lower prices. If you do not believe it will decrease sales, you can also raise prices.

Shorten payment terms. Time is money, so review the payment terms for your customer billing. Could the payment term be shortened to raise cash more quickly? Now may also be an excellent time to check for any delinquent accounts.

Prioritize and consolidate debt. If there are many different debts, it will be vital to prioritize them. For example, it is common sense to pay back high-interest-rate debt first. However, there may also be an opportunity to combine higher-interest debts with lower-interest-rate loans.

Have a target debt. Goals and metrics provide a feedback loop that helps ensure they are met. By setting a target debt and measuring it monthly, you will be better prepared to manage debt.

Reduce expenses. Perform cost-cutting with care. Ensure that any reduction in payment does not lead to negative consequences, such as a decline in quality or a loss of employee morale. It is usually best to prioritize the highest recurring costs and defer minor one-time charges.

CHAPTER **10**

Chapter 10: Project Payments

There are many ways to structure payments, so our focus will be on those that can be identified upfront. Others may arise and require tracking as the project progresses, but they will be challenging to identify up front.

An example of this is construction claims. Claims are retrospective requests to cover costs incurred that were not covered under the original scope of work, as well as similar issues involving contract wording and interpretation. For instance, in fixed-price or other contracts with cost ceilings, the buyer may demand changes that could affect the seller's ability to meet the price. These costs can be recovered through claims.

Common Project Payments

Cost-reimbursement and reimbursable-cost contracts are common payment methods for projects. In their simplest form, cost-reimbursable contracts allow contractors to bill for allowable costs plus an allowable profit. This billing is typically performed monthly, so contractors must know the allowable expenses and amounts expended each period. Likewise, the buyer will need to audit invoices more carefully to ensure that only allowable costs are included and the expected work and value are provided.

Incentive payments are often made to contractors for meeting specific targets, such as staying within a specified timeline or budget. The budget may need to include an estimate of when incentives are paid or received.

Stage payments are due upon completion of specific stages or other defined project work activities. They are often based on major WBS groupings. The project manager will need to consult the schedule for appropriate times to authorize these payments.

Many projects use payment plans that include a down payment, followed by additional progress payments or monthly payments until a certain percentage of the estimated project cost has been billed. Progress payments are typically based on milestones, so the project manager will need to consult the project schedule (and have a good one) for authorizing payments. Then, once the final project is delivered and accepted, any remaining payments are made and received.

While advance payment is less common, some suppliers may require it at the start of the project (i.e., a down payment). Others may happen as needed (e.g., at purchase).

Invoice Payment Terms

Contractors and suppliers may include various invoice payment terms. The project manager must know what these are upfront.

When immediate payment is required (also known as cash on delivery or due on receipt), the invoice should usually be paid within the billing month.

Some invoices may include the phrase "Net x," where x is usually 7, 10, 30, or 60. The number specifies how many days the invoice may be paid without incurring penalties or interest. The invoice or contract will specify what happens if that period ends and the bill remains unpaid. However, pay the invoice close to the due date without exceeding it from a time-value-of-money perspective.

Modern payment systems and transactions often allow payments to be scheduled within a specified timeframe. For example, most bill-paying systems will withdraw funds and post the transaction overnight for all parties. Payments are made within 5-7 business days to those who are not participating in the electronic payment exchange.

Another payment form is x/y Net z, where **x** is a percentage discount if the invoice is paid within **y** days. Overall, the payment is due in **z** days. For example, a 2/10 Net 30 invoice offers a 2% discount if paid within 10 days, with the payment due within 30 days. Here, some may be incentivized to reduce costs.

Finally, some invoices may be paid from a line of credit. In this case, payments may be automatic, usually within a month or quarter, as specified by the line of credit.

Cryptocurrency Payments

Cryptocurrency is an alternative currency based on decentralized computer algorithms. The defining characteristic of cryptocurrencies is that no single entity controls them. Unlike traditional currencies, cryptocurrencies are not currently regulated by governments.[11] Initially, there was considerable skepticism about cryptocurrencies compared with conventional currencies (also known as fiat currencies). However, a few governments and organizations, including financial institutions, have started accepting cryptocurrencies as a form of money.

Market forces entirely determine the value of a cryptocurrency unit, and values can fluctuate drastically (unless the currency is exchange-rate-pegged to a fiat currency). Suppose any transaction needs to be done via cryptocurrencies. In that case, the risk of exchange rate fluctuations needs to be accounted for in financial planning. In addition, many cryptocurrency transactions incur a separate transaction fee that must also be included in estimates.

While this is an option for project payments, the best practice is to plan projects in a single currency and require suppliers to submit bids and invoices in the same currency.

---

[11] While not direct regulation, the US Internal Revenue Service currently taxes the sale or exchange of cryptocurrencies and the purchase or sale of goods with cryptocurrencies (IRS 2022).

Chapter Summary

Chapter 10 explains the different ways project payments are structured and how project managers must plan for, authorize, and track them. While many payment types can be anticipated, others arise later due to scope changes or contract interpretation issues.

The chapter outlines several common payment methods:

- Cost-reimbursable contracts, where contractors bill allowable costs plus profit.
- Incentive payments tied to performance targets.
- Stage payments linked to major WBS milestones.
- Progress payments, often based on milestones or monthly billing.
- Advance payments, sometimes required by suppliers.

Project managers must understand invoice payment terms, including "Net x" deadlines, early-payment discounts (e.g., "2/10 Net 30"), and payments made through lines of credit. Paying close to, but not later than, the due date supports good cash-flow management.

The chapter concludes with a brief discussion of cryptocurrency payments, noting that while some organizations accept them, their volatility and transaction fees introduce financial risk. Best practice remains to plan projects in a single currency and require suppliers to submit bids and invoices in the same currency.

Knowledge Nuggets

Chapter Pro Tip: Due to the time value of money, pay invoices as late as possible without incurring finance charges, penalties, or other costs. Moreover, whenever possible, take an allowable discount.

Time is money, so there is an advantage to holding cash for as long as possible, especially during periods of high interest rates or dividend payouts. Pay invoices as late as possible without incurring additional charges. Consider when to make the payment based on your payment method (e.g., online transactions are usually processed overnight, and checks are generally processed within five days). Leave a small cushion for unforeseen circumstances, such as mail delays or banking holidays.

It is also wise to take any available discounts – these are usually larger than interest rates. For example, if the terms are 2/10 net 30, take the 2% discount by ensuring payment is posted by the 10th day. On the flip side, if you are billing someone, always send the bill promptly. Prompt billing means that an invoice may be paid sooner.

While your finance department may dictate changes in mitigating circumstances, these are good rules of thumb to follow for both professional and personal finance. Following this habit, you are always maximizing your investment and conserving cash.

PART III: MONITORING AND CONTROLLING COSTS (FROM EXECUTION THROUGH CLOSEOUT)

"Marketing and innovation make money. Everything else is a cost."

— Peter Drucker

CHAPTER 11

CHAPTER 11: TOOLS AND TECHNIQUES FOR COST CONTROL

As we begin to consider how to control our projects within cost allotments or address other issues, we need to understand that there are only four basic actions. The project sponsor or client will play a critical role in determining which course we take. Beyond these four basic actions, we can use additional tools throughout the project life cycle to support cost control.

Depending on factors such as project size and complexity, organizational policy, and project needs, you will need to choose one or more ways to track and analyze your budget. One method is to review each line item and note the amounts authorized, invoiced, and paid. This method is beneficial for projects involving the procurement of goods and services. Most importantly, it ensures there are no surprises. Other variances can occur when estimates are higher or lower than the authorized expenditure.

Longer-term, more complex projects also need to review planned vs. actual expenditures weekly and periodically (e.g., monthly or quarterly). Any variance between these needs to be tracked. For example, a trend of being over or under budget could be an issue requiring attention and possible corrective action.

Four Basic Execution Controls

When a project's budget is off track (overspent or underspent), there are only four essential actions to consider:

Ignore. If the problem is minor, ignoring it may be fine. A well-planned project has some tasks on, under, or at budget. In the end, these will likely even out, leaving only a slight budget variance. It is more valuable to look at trends before taking action.

Correct: The two acceptable ways to steer an off-track project back to the original plan are through crashing (adding more resources) and fast-tracking (doing more work in parallel). Both courses of action introduce additional risk, and crashing adds extra cost, which is not helpful for budgets. Fast-tracking is the practice of performing planned, budgeted work in parallel. From a budget perspective, it may be the best and only choice.

Re-plan: Here is where we may choose to change the project plan substantially. Actions may include everything from re-establishing the project baseline to de-scoping the project and agreeing that work not addressed now will be done in subsequent phases. Re-planning resets the baseline for all project parameters, including completion date, budget, and possibly scope.

Cancel: The project sponsor may, at some point, admit to failure. Admission is often a difficult decision. Sunk costs, already incurred, should not be considered. Instead, the project manager should consider using completed work to offset the loss.

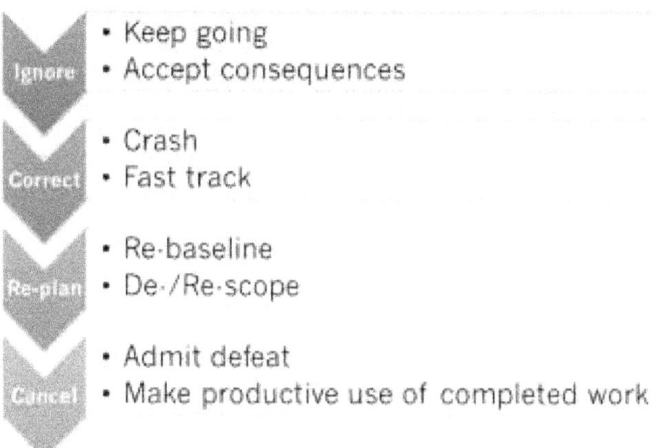

Figure 5: Four Basic Corrective Actions

Feasibility Studies

Feasibility studies assess the practicality of executing a project. Feasibility studies can encompass technical, legal, operational, scheduling, and cost feasibility.

From a financial perspective, cost feasibility determines whether the project is viable. Determining feasibility is a proactive form of cost control, which takes the following into account:

- Total estimated cost of the project
- Estimated cash flow from the project's outputs
- Finance structure of the project
- Opportunity costs due to the project

The study should also include how the feasibility of a project would change under different scenarios, such as:

- Minor or significant increases in costs
- Minor or considerable reduction of a project's financial benefits

- External factors, such as changes in economic conditions

Feasibility studies provide the project sponsor with clarity on whether to proceed. In addition, a feasibility study provides the project manager with a tool to manage costs across various scenarios proactively.

Make vs. Buy Decisions

Make vs. buy decisions are usually made by management to either manufacture a product or project component in-house or outsource the work to a supplier. Project managers and project teams may influence or be asked to participate in decision-making. The process typically starts with a cost comparison of the in-house and outsourced goods.

As with feasibility studies, costs and cost-related objectives (e.g., better cash flow management or pursuing an alternative investment) are among the reasons to decide. Typically, both quantitative and qualitative factors are considered.

Quantitative cost factors may include concrete goals such as achieving a specific unit cost. Qualitative cost factors may include spreading the investment over time or protecting intellectual property. For example, over the last decade, Apple has expanded its in-house chip-making capabilities to protect proprietary designs and gain greater control over costs and supply (Gartenberg 2021). On the other hand, construction projects often outsource labor to reduce overhead and expand the labor pool.

Budget Control Charts

Control charts are tools used to detect and mitigate quality risks. Control charts can also be used to monitor budget variance and identify trends that require corrective action.

Control charts show the upper and lower control limits (tolerance limits for variance) and how they are met over time. If a data point falls outside the upper and lower control limits, the budget is out of control or meets the Rule of Seven (and is also out of control).

The Rule of Seven states that if seven or more points are grouped consecutively together on one side of the mean, they are not random, and the process is out of control. Therefore, any data points that violate the Rule of Seven require an investigation to determine the cause of the variance. This investigation is a root cause analysis.

We can monitor other signals to conclude the process. For example, we might see unusual patterns in the data, such as ten days with little variance followed by five days with high variance. If we investigate, we may find a change on day 11 that led to this issue.

This example control chart measures weekly cost variance, measured in thousands of dollars. If the upper and lower control limits are set at $10,000 above and below the target, this budget remains within control, and no corrective action is required. On the other hand, if the limits are ± $2,000, several weeks were out of compliance, and should be investigated.

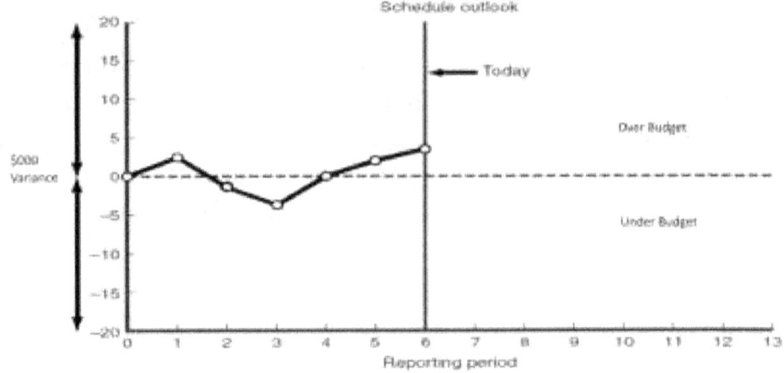

Figure 6: Budget Control Chart Example

Integrating Cost and Time

When making resource budget decisions, it is helpful to examine how the project's time and costs are progressing together. When plotting project time against cost, two shapes commonly emerge – an S-curve and a J-curve.

Many projects follow the S-curve. In this case, spending and resource expenditure start slowly, accelerate mid-project, and then slow down again. Consider, for example, the construction of an apartment building. There is extensive architectural work, other design work, permitting work, and planning. However, not many resources are involved, and cash flows out more slowly.

After the slow period, construction work finally begins. Multiple trades frame the building, provide wiring and plumbing, and close the walls. As a result, more resources and cash are consumed, making progress more visible.

As work nears completion, resource consumption and spending are slower. As a result, finishing work, inspections, and finalizing plans to open the building for leasing are taking longer, and progress is slowing again.

In contrast, some projects follow a J-curve. These projects start slowly, build momentum, and finish rapidly. Examples of J-curve projects include transformational and organizational change initiatives. As with S-curves, there is a slow start. Then changes are implemented, and once things get moving, the project progresses steadily toward completion.

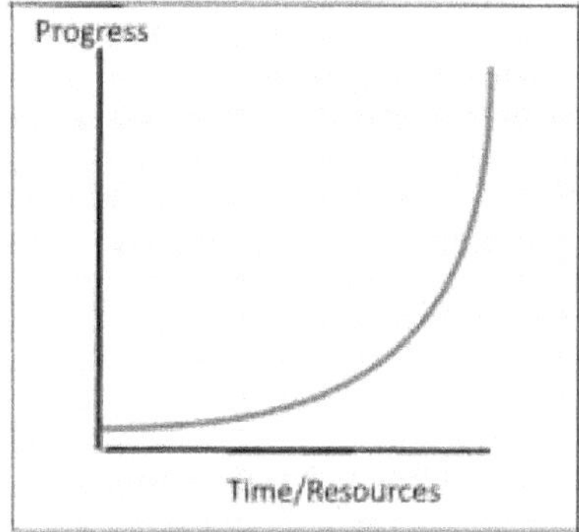

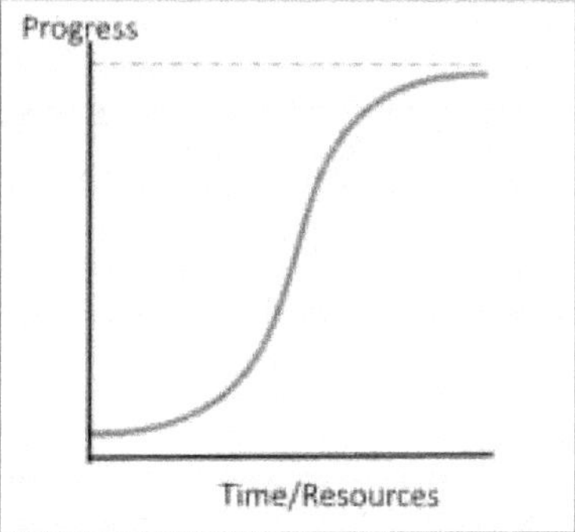

Figure 7: Project J-curve vs. S-curve

Decision-making does not require a detailed graph, just the general shape of the curve. For projects that exhibit S-curves, a top-down budgeting approach is acceptable. Modest cost-cutting and a reduced resource level are also possible without significant impact.

On the other hand, J-curve projects will likely need bottom-up budgets. Any mid-project cost or resource cuts may significantly extend the project. Cost-cutting was evident in NASA's Space Shuttle Program, which fell three years behind schedule, and

Congress then cut the budget. The impact ended with the Challenger explosion in 1986 (Meredith 2017).

Project Financial Reviews

Conduct project reviews or audits to determine adherence to project management practices and the accuracy of various project claims about the project progress. Project financial reviews or audits may be part of that process or conducted independently. A project financial review or audit aims to determine adherence to the cost management plan and verify the accuracy of project financial information.

Status meetings and reports are the norm for short-term reviews. They are about the right information, at the right time, for the right people, in the right format. The project manager must work with stakeholders to develop a communication plan that includes status reviews and reporting.

Specifically, the variance relative to the original (i.e., baseline) budget should be determined. One minor glitch does not necessarily require action. Still, analyze a downward trend or a single large deviation to determine what steps need to be taken.

Conduct project or project financial reviews as small projects. They need to have explicit initiation, planning, execution, monitoring, control, and closing. Remember, the project team members may not see the "forest for the trees." An independent review team of design or process experts might be required to examine everything entirely and objectively.

Project financial reviews may include mini-audits. Those conducting the audit need to understand the cost management controls, examine project financial documents (e.g., budgets, budget reports, invoices, and payments), and assess control risks and the accuracy of project financial documents.

The review needs to probe deeply and be "hands-on," meaning it should include site visits, questionnaires, interviews, and other facilitated meetings. Each review should end with lessons learned to ensure the review process continues to improve.

Financial Regulatory Control

It would be impractical for us to cover all financial regulations; however, some key points are worth noting. First, the US and Europe lead in defining financial regulations. Elements of their regulations may be found in many projects. Project managers should consult management and finance professionals to identify regulatory controls of concern.

Second, financial regulations impact projects in three distinct ways.

- The product or other result of the project may be subject to financial regulation, including economic sanctions.
- Financial regulations will indirectly impact how the budget and project financial reports need to be developed.
- Financial regulations will impact how the project may be financed, insurance requirements, and what occurs if the project fails.

Products across many industries and countries are subject to pricing and other economic controls. Some notable examples include oil and gas, medical devices, and pharmaceuticals. As these projects are initiated and planned, there needs to be a process to determine whether the end product is feasible within economic constraints.

Pharmaceutical projects may also need to meet specific testing requirements, which add to costs.

The International Accounting Standards Board (IASB), based in London, developed financial reporting standards. Their International Financial Reporting Standards (IFRS) are used in over 160 countries. These standards establish rules for recording financial information to ensure it is high-quality and easily comparable across organizations (Investopedia 2021). The United States and China have similar regulations: the U.S. Generally Accepted Accounting Principles (US GAAP) and the Chinese Generally Accepted Accounting Principles (Chinese GAAP) (China 2017). These standards affect financial reporting and require budget support at the lowest levels.

Finally, local laws and regulations will dictate specific project financial parameters such as:

- Interest rates that can be charged or set,
- How money may be raised in particular markets,
- What happens if a project delivers but does not meet all contractual requirements, and
- What happens if a project fails or the organization enters bankruptcy?

While previous forms of regulation change infrequently, local laws and regulations often change, including during a project. Therefore, project managers of long-term projects should monitor regulatory changes at critical intervals, such as quarterly, annually, and at the start of new project phases.

Chapter Summary

Chapter 11 focuses on the tools and techniques for controlling project costs once execution begins. Project managers ultimately have only four corrective options when budgets drift: Ignore, Correct, Re-plan, or Cancel. These actions guide teams' responses to overspending or underspending, with fast-tracking and crashing as the primary corrective techniques.

The chapter highlights feasibility studies as a proactive cost-control tool, helping determine whether a project is financially viable under different scenarios, including cost increases, benefit reductions, or economic shifts. It also explains make-vs-buy decisions, which weigh quantitative and qualitative cost factors to determine whether work should be done internally or outsourced.

Several analytical tools support cost control. Budget control charts help detect trends in variance using control limits and the Rule of Seven, prompting root-cause analysis when patterns indicate the budget is out of control. Integrating time and cost reveals S-curves and J-curves, which influence budgeting approaches and the impact of mid-project cuts.

The chapter emphasizes the importance of project financial review. Reviews should be thorough, "hands-on," and conclude with lessons learned.

Finally, the chapter outlines how financial regulations affect projects. Regulations influence how budgets are built, how financing works, and what happens if a project fails. Because local laws change frequently, long-term projects must monitor regulatory shifts regularly.

Knowledge Nuggets

Chapter Template: Budget Control Chart Template

Chapter Pro Tip: Control waste. Educate yourself about the many forms of project waste that increase costs. Then, take steps to eliminate waste.

While often thought of as "lean," agile projects can still contain waste. This waste can lead to increased project time and costs, reduced productivity, and failure to deliver the value customers expect. Much of the waste in agile projects stems from a desire for speed or time savings. Still, often the time is only postponed rather than eliminated.

Waterfall or predictive projects may be subjected to similar forms of waste. These methodologies, however, often have built-in processes and procedures to address them. As a result, some waste may only occur if these processes and procedures are ignored.

A good project manager must learn to manage and control the following ten forms of waste (and solutions) often found in projects:

- Bureaucracy - red tape will delay the team; be sure to eliminate as much bureaucracy as possible without sacrificing necessary work.
- Churn - task-switching costs in overhead; reduce the need for multi-tasking to avoid excessive churn.
- Defects and rework - doing things right the first time is best.
- Delays - delays in obtaining resources and other delays add time to value production; identify and schedule all resources in advance.
- Gold-plated product - provide what the customer needs; resist the temptation to add "bells and whistles."

- Hand-offs - handoffs cause further delays and contribute to lost knowledge; organize work to minimize handoffs and closely monitor any critical path handoffs.
- Ineffective communications - as with all projects, communication is critical.
- Lost knowledge - with minimal documentation, necessary knowledge can get lost; be sure to capture all essential documentation.
- Partially completed product - incomplete sprints or scheduled work detract from delivering value; keep all work on track.
- Unplanned localization - not just for software projects, unplanned localization is time-consuming; consider localization needs during planning and not as an afterthought.

Take some time to review this list and consider how you will avoid these areas of waste in your next project.

CHAPTER 12

Chapter 12: An Introduction to Earned Value Management

Imagine you are the project manager for a project to lay four miles of highway in four weeks with a $1 million budget per week. Now, assume that only $2 million was spent after three weeks. How is the project doing?

You might be suspicious because you have heard that large projects always go over budget, but does that mean the project is performing poorly? The truth is YOU DO NOT KNOW! Knowing how much money was spent is one piece of the puzzle, but how much work was done? Are there three miles of highway? Or perhaps only two?

If I do not tell you the cost but tell you three miles of highway are ready, you are no better off. Measuring project progress requires examining the triple constraint of cost, schedule, and scope.

To assess a project's status accurately (and apply proper project control), you need to examine the relationship among cost, schedule, and scope. These three are the standard, trackable project constraints (i.e., the triple constraints). Therefore, it would be best to convert each to standard units for an apples-to-apples comparison. Earned Value Management can help by converting all three to a common currency-based unit.

Basic Concepts

In Earned Value Management, the schedule and scope are converted to dollars or other currency units to compare the plan to the budget. Once converted, it is possible to examine variance (i.e., the difference between the plan and the actual) and forecast project completion.

Three basic terms support this conversion to measure variance, and forecast costs and schedule. They are:

Term	Meaning
Planned Value (PV)	The value of work planned to complete in a period is measured by the budget for the work
Earned Value (EV)	The value earned is the budgeted cost of the completed work
Actual Cost (AC)	The amount spent to achieve the work that has already been done

Table 3: Essential Earned Value Management Terms[12,13]

[12] PV was formerly known as Budgeted Cost of Work Scheduled (BCWS).
[13] EV was formerly known as Budgeted Cost of Work Performed (BCWP).

Earned value (EV) answers the question, "How much of the planned work have we actually completed, expressed in budgeted dollars?" In practice, EV is determined through these steps:

- Identify the total budget for the activity or work package.
- Assess how much of the work has actually been completed (using physical percent complete, milestones, weighted steps, or another approved method).
- Multiply the percent complete by the budgeted amount.

For example, if a task has a $1 million budget and is 40% complete, then EV = 0.40 × $1 million = $400 thousand. That $400 thousand represents the value of work completed to date, expressed in planned dollars.

Small, less complex projects can typically determine all the measurements accurately. However, larger, more complex projects may elect to credit the value earned as a percentage of the project completion percentage or use other allocation methods.

Determining percent complete is one of the most challenging steps in Earned Value Management. Because earned value is based on the budgeted value of completed work, the method used to assess progress must be consistent, objective, and appropriate for the type of work being measured. Several standard techniques are used across industries:

- **Physical Percent Complete**: The team estimates how much of the work has been physically completed. This method works best for tangible, measurable deliverables such as construction, manufacturing, or engineering tasks. Example: 3 of 5 components installed = 60% complete.

- **Milestone Method:** Work is broken into measurable milestones, each assigned a portion of the budget. Earned value is credited only when a milestone is fully achieved. Example: "Design Approved" milestone earns 40% of the work package budget.

- **Weighted Steps Method**: Similar to milestones, but each step is assigned a weight based on its importance or effort. This method is practical when tasks have predictable internal stages. Example: Drafting (20%), Review (30%), Finalization (50%).

- **0/100 or 50/50 Method**: No earned value is credited until the work is fully complete, or 50% is earned when work begins, and the remaining 50% is earned when it is completed. The 0/100 method is ideal for short-duration tasks or tasks where partial credit would be misleading. Example: A 10-day task earns 50% on day 1 and 50% on completion.

- **Level of Effort (LOE):** Used for support or administrative activities that do not produce discrete deliverables. Earned value is credited evenly over time. Example: Monthly project reporting earns EV at a steady rate.

Let us see how this works for our highway project. We will also assume the same level of effort has been applied weekly throughout the construction. At the end of the third week, the planned value (PV) will be $3 million. So that is $1 million for each week. Earned value is the value of completed work relative to the budget.

Suppose there were 2.5 miles of finished road. That would make the earned value (EV) $2.5 million. The actual cost (AC) was $2 million.

Cost and Schedule Variance

To summarize, at the end of the third week, we have:

PV = $3 million, the value of the work that should be done

EV = $2.5 million, the value of the work done

AC = $2 million, the money already spent

Now we can find our cost (CV) and schedule (SV) variance through two simple formulas:

CV = EV – AC, compares the value earned with the money spent, regardless of the schedule

SV = EV – PV, compares the value earned with the value planned to be achieved by now, regardless of the money spent

Equation 13: Cost and Schedule Variance

Suppose CV or SV is equal to 0. In that case, the project is right on target, and there is no variance, an improbable scenario. Any negative numbers are overruns (we are overspending on time and schedule), and positive numbers are underruns (we are underspending on time and schedule). For our sample project, the variances would be:

CV = $2.5 million - $2 million = $0.5 million (ahead of budget)

SV = \$2.5 million - \$3 million = (\$0.5 million) (behind schedule)

Cost and Schedule Performance Index

While knowing the variance is helpful, we do not always need to act on unfavorable variances. Some project work will be early, and some will be late. Some work will cost more, and some will be less. We should be interested in large spikes or worsening trends.

Once we determine the schedule and cost variance, we can also compute the variance rate over time. The rate will help identify trends and make forecasts. We use the cost performance index (CPI) and the schedule performance index (SPI). Calculate them as:

CPI = EV ÷ AC, the ratio of earned value to costs

SPI = EV ÷ PV, the ratio of earned value to schedule

Equation 14: Cost and Schedule Performance Indices

In this case, a value of 1 means the project is right on target. Values greater than 1 are underruns, and values less than 1 are overruns.

Tip: It is easy to remember the variance and index formulas because they

- always start with earned value (EV)
- variance formulas use subtraction (i.e., -)
- index formulas change the minus sign of the variance formulas to a division sign (i.e., ÷).

Back to our example, we have:

CPI = \$2.5 million ÷ \$2 million = 1.25, an underrun

SPI = \$2.5 million ÷ \$3 million = 0.83, an overrun

These can be interpreted as:

We are achieving \$1.25 in value per dollar spent (125%), keeping us under budget.

We are achieving 0.83 hours of completed work per hour of effort (83%), resulting in a schedule overage.

Cost Forecasting

A few additional terms and formulas are now needed for cost forecasting. We will focus on costs to avoid complexity, and similar calculations are available for schedules. They are:

Term	Meaning
Budget at Completion (BAC)	The authorized project budget
Estimate at Completion (EAC)	What the total expenditure will be at the project's end
Estimate to Complete (ETC)	The amount of money needed to complete the project from the current situation
Variance at Completion (VAC)	The difference between the authorized budget (BAC) and what we forecast it will take (EAC)

Table 4: Additional Earned Value Management Terms for Forecasting

Suppose the CPI or SPI is the same over time. This lack of change is a warning that a past issue remains uncorrected. In other words, we may be working at 125% of the budget, and we will remain at that level.

In this case, compute the estimate at completion as:

EAC = BAC / CPI, the ratio of the authorized budget to the cost performance index

Equation 15: Estimate at Completion

The stated budget for the project at completion is $4 million. Substituting the values:

EAC = $4 million / 1.25 = $3.2 million

The EAC indicates that the expected total expenditure at the end of the project will be $3.2 million, $0.8 million less than the authorized budget.

Also:

$$ETC = EAC - AC$$

$$VAC = BAC - EAC$$

Equation 16: Estimate to Complete and Variance at Completion

Again, substituting the values:

ETC = $3.2 million - $2 million = $1.2 million

This ETC indicates we need to spend an additional $1.2 million to complete the project. And:

$$VAC = \$4 \text{ million} - \$3.2 \text{ million} = \$0.8 \text{ million}$$

The difference between the authorized budget and the forecast end-of-project budget is $0.8 million in savings.

Suppose the CPI or SPI grows over time or varies significantly. More severe issues may be at play, and there are better formulas for computing the EAC. In this case, other procedures can be used to calculate the EAC, but they are beyond the scope of this introduction.

These forecasts also allow the project manager to determine if catching up and meeting the original budget (or timeline) is feasible. The to-complete performance index (TCPI) compares the value of the remaining work to the remaining budget. TCPI allows us to determine if we can meet the estimate at completion (EAC) and the rate of change required to meet it:

$$TCPI = (BAC - EV) / (BAC - AC)$$

Equation 17: To Complete Performance Index

For the hypothetical project, this is:

$$TCPI = (\$4 \text{ million} - \$2.5 \text{ million}) / (\$4 \text{ million} - \$2 \text{ million}) = \$1.5 \text{ million} / \$2 \text{ million} = 0.75$$

To meet the EAC (which is lower than the BAC), we need to spend only 75% of the budget for the project's remaining time.

Now, we need to compare TCPI with CPI. It should be easy to catch up if they are close in value. However, if the TCPI exceeds the CPI, the BAC may be understated. Similarly, if the TCPI is less than the CPI, the BAC may be overstated. However, unless the scope of work has an approved increase, the BAC must not change; other variables must adjust accordingly.

Finally, the more significant the difference between the CPI and the TCPI, the less likely the project is to catch up (PMI 2021). Furthermore, it may be impossible to catch up if this difference is not detected during the first 15% of the delivery schedule (Lewis 2011).

To conclude the hypothetical problem, since the TCPI and CPI differ by only .5 and there is a budget underrun, it should be easy to adjust spending to meet the authorized budget. However, catching up would be less likely if the difference were larger.

Chapter Summary

Chapter 12 introduces Earned Value Management (EVM) as a method for measuring project performance by integrating cost, schedule, and scope into a single, comparable unit of measure. The chapter emphasizes that knowing only cost or only progress is insufficient, noting that you do not know how a project is performing without examining all three constraints together.

EVM relies on three foundational metrics: **Planned Value (PV), Earned Value (EV)**, and **Actual Cost (AC)**. EV is calculated by multiplying the percent complete by the budgeted amount, making the accuracy of percent-complete assessments critical. The chapter outlines several standard methods: physical percent complete, milestones, weighted steps, 0/100 or 50/50, and level of effort.

Using these values, project managers calculate **Cost Variance (CV)** and **Schedule Variance (SV)**, with positive values indicating underruns and negative values indicating overruns. Performance indices—CPI and SPI—convert these variances into efficiency ratios, showing how effectively the project is using time and money.

Forecasting tools such as **Estimate at Completion (EAC)**, **Estimate to Complete (ETC)**, **Variance at Completion (VAC)**, and the **To-Complete Performance Index (TCPI)** are introduced. These help determine whether the project can still meet its budget and how efficiently remaining work must be performed. As the text notes, a widening gap between CPI and TCPI signals that "it may be impossible to catch up."

Overall, EVM provides a structured, quantitative way to assess performance, identify trends, and forecast outcomes, making it one of the most powerful tools in cost control.

- **Formulas**: Cost variance (CV), schedule variance (SV), cost performance index (CPI), schedule performance index (SPI), estimate at completion (EAC), estimate to complete (ETC), variance at completion (VAC), and to complete performance index (TCPI)

Knowledge Nuggets

Chapter Pro Tip: If possible, use a simplified Earned Value Management approach for status updates. Stakeholders who appreciate detailed status will embrace these.

While the full practice of EVM can be complex, it also offers a simple way to update clients on the status of smaller projects. However, before we look at the "how," let us look at the "how often."

The frequency will depend on many factors, but we recommend starting with once a week. If a month passes and a problem arises, it is usually too late to do anything. Once a week allows you to keep a closer track of expenditures and invoices. Once a week, it also lets the client see progress. Of course, you can always skip reporting for a week if you did not work on the project, but you still need to continue tracking expenditures and invoices. Log expenditures, invoices, and payments to get the full picture of the project.

Your weekly client report needs to include the basics of cost and schedule variances, plus an estimate of remaining expenses. Knowing the cost and schedule indices is not necessarily of interest to a client. Still, it helps assess project health. Rather than include it, you might use it in a formula to color-code the data. A basic format to use for clients is:

	PV	EV	AC	SV	CV	ETC
Project 1	$0	$0	$0	$0	$0	$1.5M
Change Request 1	7,456	6,128	7,400	(1,328)	(1,272)	100K
Totals	$7,456	$6,128	$7,400	($1,328)	($1,272)	$1.6M

Figure 8: EVMS Status Reporting Format

Note that the projects and change requests are listed separately. In this case, a project has not started yet. However, a change request has. The condition might indicate that the client forgot to complete a significant task the team needed to complete before the project began.

The client can see the weekly progress of planned vs. actual expenditures. At the start of the status reporting, include a legend for the columns. A simple footnote under the table explains any significant deviations. Clients see what is happening from week to week; there are no surprises.

You could slightly improve this by color-coding by index. Anything around 1.0 is good. Anything too large may be too good to be true, and anything less than .9 may indicate an issue requiring action. You can decide the actual performance specifications based on how tightly you need to control the project.

CHAPTER 13

Chapter 13: Contracts and Work Authorization Systems

Our purpose here is not to provide legal advice or fully define contracts, but to examine them to the extent they contribute to cost control. While contract law differs from country to country, the basic principles of US contract law are generally more comprehensive. Moreover, they cover many regulations prevalent in other countries, though perhaps interpreted differently.

Contract Basics

A US contract document must contain these elements to be considered legally binding, valid, and enforceable:

- **Offer** – There must be an offer made to provide goods or services
- **Acceptance** – The offer must be accepted
- **Consideration** – There must be an exchange of something tangible in return for the products or services. The deal could be in the form of money, property, or other services.

- **Capacity** – Those signing the document must be legally able to do so.
- **Intent** – There must be intent to enter a contract. The intent is usually evident when the agreement is written, and the facts are stated correctly.
- **Object** – The object of the contract must be legal. A contract to purchase illegal drugs or provide services for illegal immigrants is not a binding contract.

While many legal systems permit oral or implied contracts, doing so is not recommended in a project environment.

Other Contract Considerations

In general, all contracts should also include the following for clarity:

- The start date and length of the term for which the agreement will remain valid
- A detailed offer to provide goods or services and the details of pricing or consideration.
- Memorialize all promises in the contract – do not take things for granted.
- Any payment terms should be spelled out and include the mailing addresses for invoices and payments.
- Approved signatures of those able to bind the organization to a contract
- Agree on one set of rules if multiple jurisdictions with differing laws are involved

In addition, many contracts now include mediation or arbitration clauses to avoid lengthy court proceedings.

Contracts may also include additional standard and special clauses that specify the terms and conditions of the agreement. Terms and conditions can impact payments and costs, so project managers should know the ones in their contracts. Some standard terms and conditions include (but are not limited to):

- **Acceptance**: what constitutes acceptable work, often a primary source of delay if not well defined
- **Bonds**: purchased payment or performance guarantees
- **Breach/Default:** what occurs if obligations are not met
- **Changes**: how contractual changes may be made
- **Confidentiality**: what information can or cannot be shared
- **Force Majeure**: what happens in the event of an "act of God" (e.g., an earthquake)
- **Intellectual Property**: specifies who owns the work
- **Notice**: determines who receives contract communications
- **Payments**: detailed information on timing and amounts of payments
- **Termination or Exit**: establishes how a project can be canceled or abandoned before the contract is complete
- **Warranties**: promises of quality for goods and services, usually with limited periods

Regardless of your locale, contracts rely heavily on good faith, the parties' good intentions, and trust. When these are broken, pursuing mediation or arbitration can help preserve the relationship between the parties.

Contract Types

There are four primary types of contracts, each with advantages and disadvantages. They are fixed-price, time-and-materials, cost-reimbursement, and incentive.

Fixed-price contracts have the agreed-upon value negotiated upfront. The buyer's advantage is that the project's budget is known upfront. On the other hand, sellers or contractors must plan carefully, as they bear the risk of delays and failures. As a result, sellers will likely demand more detailed project requirements and specifications before agreeing to a contract. The statement of work needs much more detail.

Failures of fixed-price contracts may lead to complex negotiations. For example, a buyer could not comply with all the terms and supply everything they agreed to on time. On the other hand, the seller was hired for a specific area of expertise. They could not provide all the necessary resources at the specified times either. As a result, the six-month contract was extended beyond a year, after which the seller returned to request additional payment. Finally, additional payment was negotiated, and the project was completed in 18 months; both parties were pleased with the results.

Time-and-materials contracts are generally best for short-term work and are often used for staff augmentation. Here, the client or buyer absorbs the risk. They need a budget to cover the work and may have to negotiate a larger one if the project does not meet their needs. Many large enterprise software projects start as time-and-materials contracts with a short-term expectation. In some instances, a lack of in-house experience and project complexity often lead to higher costs and longer timelines. The primary variable here is labor hours, so the client needs to manage the work more closely to ensure that all goals are met. These goals may include transferring knowledge to internal staff to reduce reliance on outside labor.

Cost-reimbursement contracts allow payment of authorized, negotiated costs. These are often used in nonprofit and facilities contracts, such as building maintenance and services. They may also be used to specify research and development projects. The contractor or seller bears much of the risk and must have a sound cost accounting system to track costs and ensure they are allowable. The client or buyer also needs to monitor carefully. There are several variations of this contract type.

A cost-plus percentage-of-cost contract is not allowable in many government situations. When a vendor has their costs covered and an additional profit on each expense, there is insufficient incentive for the vendor to control costs reasonably. Adding an incentive, an award (a payment made upon contract award), or an additional fixed fee is more acceptable.

Incentives can take many forms and should be designed to achieve the desired outcomes. In particular, they can:

- Reward positive and extraordinary efforts
- Accelerate the delivery schedule
- Reduce delays by encouraging proactive risk mitigation
- Discourage waste

For example, a tight budget might incentivize meeting project financial goals. Those with shorter timelines may incentivize meeting specific goals or delivery targets. However, incentives must be carefully planned. Poorly designed incentives can distort behavior, for example, by accelerating delivery at the expense of budget and quality.

Maintaining a specific date can also be important. For example, maintenance tasks may need to begin before the project ends (e.g., road repairs, repainting). They may require revenues to fund that work as soon as possible to minimize additional project costs.

There is no reason multiple incentives cannot be used. Incentives may also be on a sliding scale. For example, the buyer may offer a 20% bonus to meet a budget item, or a 10% bonus for being a small amount under budget.

Contract Selection for Cost Control

Familiarity with the basic contract types and their advantages and disadvantages is essential for cost control. Selecting the appropriate contract type can significantly affect project outcomes. Procurement is much more complex and is a separate project management knowledge area. Still, appropriate contract choices will help meet project cost goals.

You must work closely with your company's finance or procurement specialists to ensure projects are delivered and to design successful contract negotiations that build relationships. Correct contract choices will help those in the relationship stay "on the same page" and achieve common goals.

Here is a table summarizing the advantages and disadvantages. Added incentives steer the outcomes further.

Contract Type	Advantages	Disadvantages
Fixed Price	• Less work for buyer to manage • Seller motivated to control costs • Total budget known up front	• Needs buyer to write detailed scope • Seller may not complete work if losing money • Seller may deliberately under price or under scope to profit from change orders
Cost Reimbursement	• Lower cost than fixed price since seller doesn't need to manage risk as closely	• Total price is unknown • Requires auditing of invoices creating more work to manage • Only moderate incentive to control time and costs
Time & Materials	• Quick to create • Usually short duration • Good choice for staff augmentation	• Seller profits from every hour, hence no cost or time control incentive • Requires most buyer oversight, but least buyer start up time • Total price may be unknown
Incentive (one of above with added incentive)	• Keeps everyone on the same page • Helps achieve goals and targets • The advantages of the chosen type	• The disadvantages of the chosen type • Additional cost to cover the incentive

Table 5: Contract Type Comparison

Work Authorization Systems

While contracts establish the external framework for cost control, work authorization systems provide the internal mechanism to ensure work proceeds according to plan. A work authorization system is a formal mechanism that can be implemented manually or with application support. It ensures project work begins only when the required conditions are met. It links the schedule baseline to the actual release of work, preventing teams from starting tasks prematurely, out of sequence, or without the necessary approvals, resources (including funding), or information. By controlling when work can begin, the system helps maintain budget and schedule integrity and supports accurate performance measurement. This is especially important in earned value environments.

Work authorization typically begins with a review to ensure prerequisites are met, such as that predecessor tasks are complete, resources are available, funding is allocated, and the scope is approved. This step ensures that work does not begin until the project is ready to support it. Once the conditions are satisfied, a formal authorization is issued. This may take the form of a work order, a work package release, a digital authorization within a project management system, or a simple “go” from the project manager. The authorization specifies the scope of work, the responsible individual or team, the planned start and finish dates, and any constraints or dependencies that must be observed.

As work progresses, a formal authorization system continues to play a role by tracking compliance and monitoring progress. Unauthorized work is prevented, thereby maintaining alignment with the schedule baseline. This is especially important in environments using earned value, where out-of-sequence work can distort performance metrics. When the work is completed or when circumstances change, the authorization is closed, updated, or reissued. This creates a clear, auditable trail of decisions and approvals that supports both governance and accountability.

Work authorization systems contribute significantly to financial success. By ensuring work begins only as planned, they preserve the schedule's logic, reduce the risk of out-of-sequence activities that could delay the project, and ensure only planned expenditures are made. They also prevent scope creep by ensuring that only approved work is released. Because work is authorized based on resource availability, the system improves coordination, optimizes resource usage, and reduces bottlenecks. Perhaps most importantly, it supports the accuracy of earned-value and earned-schedule calculations. When work starts and finishes according to plan, performance metrics reflect the project's actual behavior rather than uncontrolled activity.

Agile and hybrid teams also support a simplified work authorization process. Although less formal, these mechanisms serve the same purpose: ensuring that only approved work is executed. Prioritizing stories in the product backlog and assigning them to specific iterations or sprints creates the expectation that only those stories will be worked on. Stories are not added to iterations until all requirements are clear and all acceptance criteria are defined.

Despite these benefits, work authorization systems are not without drawbacks. When implemented with excessive formality, too many approvers, or too many approval conditions, they can slow execution and frustrate teams. Teams in agile and creative environments may view formal work release as too restrictive.

Even with these challenges, the advantages of a well-designed work authorization system are substantial. It strengthens project governance, enhances predictability, and provides a structured way to ensure work is completed on time, within budget, by the right people, and under the right conditions. When used thoughtfully, it becomes a powerful tool for maintaining schedule discipline and supporting successful project delivery.

Chapter Summary

Contracts and work authorization systems play a critical role in cost control. Contracts establish the legal and operational framework for project work, defining obligations, deadlines, deliverables, and the allocation of risk between buyers and sellers. Understanding the essential elements of a contract (offer, acceptance, consideration, capacity, intent, and legality) helps project managers recognize what makes an agreement enforceable and how contractual clarity supports predictable execution. Terms and conditions, such as acceptance criteria, change procedures, warranties, and force majeure provisions, further shape how work is performed and how schedules and their risks are managed.

Different contract types influence schedule performance in different ways. Fixed-price contracts shift schedule risk to the seller, often requiring detailed specifications and careful planning. Time-and-materials contracts shift risk to the buyer and require close oversight to prevent schedule drift. Cost-reimbursement contracts demand strong cost controls and monitoring, while incentive contracts use financial rewards to motivate timely delivery or exceptional performance. Selecting the right contract type and designing appropriate incentives can significantly improve financial and schedule outcomes.

Work authorization systems complement contractual controls by regulating when work may begin. They ensure that tasks start only when prerequisites are met, resources are available, and the scope is complete and approved. By preventing out-of-sequence work and unauthorized activity, work-authorization systems protect the schedule baseline and support accurate performance measurement, especially in earned-value and earned-schedule environments. Even agile and hybrid teams use simplified forms of work authorization through backlog prioritization and sprint planning. When implemented thoughtfully, work authorization systems strengthen governance, reduce schedule risk, and help teams deliver work predictably and efficiently.

Knowledge Nuggets

Chapter Pro Tip: Contracts can reveal what aspects of the project are most important. Incentive clauses in contracts can keep everyone on the same page.

A well-written contract should reveal what aspects of a project are most important. The important items will usually revolve around one of the constraints: time, cost, quality, or scope. If you are writing a contract, consider adding an incentive clause or taking future actions to encourage meeting the most critical goals. If you are negotiating a contract, you may want to request an incentive clause.

A perfect example comes from the construction of the Øresund Link, a bridge-tunnel connecting Sweden and Denmark. When the project began, the intent was to maintain an end date ten years in the future to coincide with a celebratory day. However, by the time the project was two to three years from completion, risk management estimated less than a 25% chance of meeting the end date.

Normal schedule risk responses, such as searching for additional work to do in parallel, were implemented. In addition, the consortium managing the project offered a significant bonus, to be shared by all contractors, if the end date was met, to incentivize completion. Finally, on 1 July 2000, the Link was officially opened, meeting the goal set ten years earlier.

CHAPTER **14**

Chapter 14: Project Cash Flow Management

Project budgets within an organization only tell part of the story. Budgets inform the need for committed funds. However, they do not indicate when actual cash is received or when payments are due. Cash may need to be planned as a resource for many large, complex projects.

Cash Flow Concepts

For many projects, it is not just about costs and payments. For example, financing for large projects may require disbursing loan funds to the organization over time. Alternatively, suppose you are building a mixed-use tower. The customer may pay you, as the general contractor, an advance monthly fee for certain work. The idea is that these payments will help cover some of your expenses while you run the project. Cash will both flow in and flow out.

Suppose you work for an organization that uses in-house human resources and has a central procurement department to obtain materials. In that case, this may not be a concern. However, for large construction projects, for example, where most work is performed by contractors, not having these plans and commitments in place can mean the difference between success and failure. For example, if a contractor expects payment and your Finance Department says, "Sorry, we do not have the cash," the contractor may withhold work or materials.

Cash Flow Forecasts

A cash flow forecast is time-phased, usually by month. It is an estimate of the actual cash required. Cash used in financial transactions can include legal tender, checks, bank drafts, money orders, and demand deposit accounts. Cash can also include digital payments and technologies (Investopedia 2026). Let us look at a simple example of cash flow from personal finances.

You plan to purchase a replacement air filter online for $20 in September and include it in your budget for that month. You buy it on September 15 and decide to pay by credit card. You budgeted the purchase for September, but the invoice is not due immediately.

Suppose you receive a credit card bill for your billing cycle on October 10. It states that you have 25 days to pay without interest or penalty. Actual cash, therefore, is not required until November, when you pay the bill via your checking account.

Now, let us look at a variation. You have $20 available for the air filter budget in September. A day before you purchase the filter, a friend gives you a $20 gift card for your birthday. So you have a cash inflow of $20. When you order the air filter, you enter the gift card number as payment, resulting in a $20 cash outflow. For the air filter, the net cash requirement was $0.

By understanding money's payment terms and time value, you can think through every cost and determine the cash flow forecast. Having a good cash flow forecast will reduce business and financial risks. Companies need to monitor cash flow closely. Many have gone bankrupt, focusing only on incoming revenue and not on spending. At the same time, your organization will perform better financially, with each expenditure being more carefully planned and managed.

In the following figure, the net cash is negative, indicating that more cash is needed. A negative amount indicates the need to borrow funds or to draw on the organization's operations or treasury to cover the costs.

Cash Flow Forecast

Month	*Cash In*	*Cash Out*
September		
- contractor payments due		$50,000
- lumber purhase (down payment)		10,000
- August training courses		5,000
- progress payment received	20,000	
September Net Cash	($45,000)	

Figure 9: Sample Cash Flow

Chapter Summary

Chapter 14 introduces **project cash flow management**, emphasizing that budgets alone do not show when money is actually needed. Cash flow planning becomes essential for large, contractor-heavy, or loan-financed projects.

The chapter explains that cash flows include both **inflows** (such as customer advance payments or loan disbursements) and **outflows** (such as contractor invoices, materials, and labor). Without proper planning, a project may face delays if payments cannot be made when due. Contractors may even halt work if there isn't sufficient cash to pay them.

A **cash flow forecast** is time-phased, usually monthly, and estimates when cash must actually be paid. The chapter uses a personal finance example to illustrate how payment timing differs from budgeting: a purchase budgeted in September may not require cash until November, depending on billing cycles. Cash inflows, such as gift cards or customer advances, also affect net cash requirements.

Ultimately, cash flow forecasting helps reduce financial risk, prevent liquidity problems, and ensure the organization can meet obligations as they arise. A negative cash flow position signals the need for borrowing or internal funding support.

Knowledge Nuggets

Chapter Template: Cash Flow Template

Chapter Pro Tip: Applying cash flow concepts to your personal and business finances will help you succeed.

Cash flow is the cash that enters and leaves your accounts over time. Monitoring cash flow ensures that funds are available to meet financial obligations, such as debt repayment and operating expenses. Over time, strive to create excess cash. This extra cash can provide working capital to fund additional projects.

Cash flow will also help you understand how funds are spent. The information will help create better budgets and support longer-term planning. Furthermore, it will help set aside funds for future expenses or projects. Finally, monitoring cash flow will help determine the payment terms to offer buyers or clients to cover the costs of providing goods and services.

Going forward, do not just focus on revenue or profit. There have been profitable companies that lost customers and suppliers and entered bankruptcy because they failed to manage cash flow effectively.

CHAPTER 15

Chapter 15: Cost Management and Project Closeout

Their project sponsors and clients usually remember project managers for their project delivery and approach to closeout. Achieving a high level of satisfaction requires attention to many details, including:

- Ensuring that all requirements have been met and planning remedies if they are not
- Organizing acceptance test results and meetings to review them
- Documenting any known issues from testing
- Demonstrating the project and preparing for a turnover
- Seeing if the sponsor or client feels additional testing is necessary
- Preparing final copies of requirements, designs, training materials, user guides, operational information, and anything else promised
- Providing support during the transition period

Many project managers forget that each of these activities has an associated cost. If these activities are not planned and scheduled, it may be easy to exceed budgets during project closeout. In addition, project financial closure itself has associated costs for activities.

Project Termination or Suspension

Project managers also need to understand that a project can end in four ways, each of which may affect project costs. Therefore, consider the type of project termination when planning and executing project closure. These ways are:

Addition. Projects developed internally, yet independently, and successfully are made a formal part of the developing organization to play their role. For example, a university creates an extended studies division that operates independently yet remains part of the university.

Extinction. A project succeeds or fails. A successful project achieves its goals and benefits and is turned over to the project sponsor or client for operations. Unsuccessful projects fail to meet their goals. For example, a developed medical product does not meet regulatory requirements, cannot proceed, and the company decides it is infeasible to replan.

Integration. Successful projects are commonly embedded and integrated into the chartering organization. These activities can be time-consuming and should be budgeted, if possible.

Starvation. For various business or legal reasons, funds and resources may be withheld or withdrawn rather than end a project. After a period, the project may be terminated altogether.

Termination by murder is a variation in which the shutdown is sudden and without warning.

Projects may also be suspended, a state that also implies costs. For example, if a construction project runs out of funding, the work may need to be halted temporarily. Work completed to date may require protection (e.g., a security guard or secure storage of unused resources) until additional funding is secured.

Project Financial Closure Planning

Financial closure comprises the steps required to confirm that all work has been completed and paid for. Improperly executed project financial closure can create legal issues related to contracts and payments. In some cases, a termination project manager is tasked explicitly with closing out the project. Therefore, the project manager should plan all financial closure activities during the project planning phase. Omitting anything can cause a scramble during the last days of the project to close gaps.

Typical financial closure activities requiring cost and schedule planning include:

Administrative Activities

Administrative activities ensure that the project's records, schedule data, and lessons learned are complete, accurate, and ready for organizational use.

- Verifying that all scheduled activities, milestones, and deliverables have been completed as planned and ensuring formal project sign-off.
- Reviewing the project schedule to ensure alignment with project objectives and completion of all tasks.

- Updating budget and schedule data to reflect actual start and finish dates, as well as documenting any variances from the original schedule baseline for historical purposes.
- Comparing the approved budget and schedule baseline to actual performance to identify variances and include insights in the final report and for lessons learned.
- Allocating time for lessons learned sessions, archiving project information, and preparing closure documentation.
- Ensuring any schedule management issues are a part of lessons learned.
- Performing team evaluations.

Contractual and Financial Activities

Contractual and financial activities ensure that all agreements, payments, and obligations are fully resolved, enabling the project to close without lingering liabilities or delays.

- Reviewing contracts for compliance and ensuring signed copies are retained.
- Reviewing all invoices and payments.
- Complying with any remaining financing terms and transitioning from project financing to operational financing.
- Identifying outstanding invoices or other required payments and arranging payment.
- Receiving any final payments due.
- Selling unnecessary equipment and materials or returning them to an appropriate location or individual.
- Conducting a final financial audit.

Operational Activities

Operational activities focus on transferring the project's outputs into the organization's operational environment, ensuring that deliverables are ready for use and that resources are released efficiently.

- Facilitating the transition of deliverables to operations, maintenance, or another team, as outlined in the schedule. Some organizations may have formal steps that must be followed to ensure quality and protect the operational environment. Some organizations also require a formal benefits handover or a benefits-tracking plan to ensure that the project's expected outcomes can be measured after closeout.
- Releasing resources as early as possible to avoid additional costs.
- Confirming operational acceptance.
- Ensuring support teams are prepared.

Project Financial Closure

Financial closure offers immediate benefits. Legal issues are avoided, and the actual project cost can be calculated. However, all contractual and regulatory requirements must be met during the process. Therefore, now is the time to follow the closure plan carefully.

Project financial closure must be completed in full and promptly to avoid unnecessary expenditures. In addition, the project organization's finance department may rely on the closure to prepare necessary reports, arrange additional operational financing, and adjust financial statements. So be sure to meet their requirements as well.

Once the project is closed, it is best to have a final sign-off. "This is rarely done in projects, but [we] strongly recommend having a specific close-out document, signed by both parties, that the contract [*or project*] has been formally ended and that all obligations have been met, except long-term obligations that are listed in the document, including post-project services and warranties (Lehmann 2019)."

It is important to note that the end of a project can be an emotional time for all concerned. Some people may be wondering about their next job. There may be a fear of ending friendships and other relationships, and the project may have become a way of life for many. While sensitivity is required, it does not hinder the project's financial closure.

Closeout Best Practices

Effective project closeout requires the same level of discipline and planning applied to other project work. One of the most important best practices is to begin planning for closure during project planning. By identifying closure activities in advance and including them in the budget and schedule, project managers avoid last-minute scrambling and ensure that time and resources are available to complete all required tasks.

Another best practice is to maintain accurate and up-to-date project records throughout execution. When schedules, contracts, financial data, and deliverable documentation are up to date, closeout becomes far more efficient. Teams can quickly verify completion, identify outstanding items, and prepare final reports without reconstructing historical data. This also supports accurate lessons learned and strengthens organizational knowledge.

Clear communication with stakeholders is essential during closeout. Project sponsors, clients, operations teams, and vendors must understand what remains to be done, what documentation they will receive, and when responsibilities will transfer. Early engagement with operations or maintenance teams helps ensure that they are prepared to accept deliverables, reducing the risk of post-handover disruptions.

Finally, successful closeout requires attention to the human side of project work. Team members may feel uncertain about future assignments or reluctant to leave a long-running project. Acknowledging these emotions, celebrating accomplishments, and providing clarity about next steps can help maintain morale and ensure that closure activities are completed thoroughly and professionally.

Chapter Summary

Chapter 15 explains how cost management continues through project closeout, emphasizing that sponsors often remember project managers by how well they finish a project. Closeout activities such as acceptance testing, documentation, turnover, and transition support all carry costs. If these activities are not planned and scheduled, it may be easy to exceed budgets during project closeout.

The chapter outlines four ways projects can end: **addition**, **extinction**, **integration**, and **starvation**, each with different cost implications. Projects may also be suspended, which can create ongoing expenses such as security, storage, or maintenance of partially completed work.

Effective closeout requires financial closure planning, including verifying deliverables, reviewing contracts and invoices, resolving outstanding payments, conducting audits, and transitioning financing to operations. Operational closeout includes transferring deliverables, releasing resources, and ensuring support teams are ready.

The chapter stresses that project financial closure must be completed fully and promptly. Delays can create legal issues and disrupt organizational financial reporting. A formal closeout document signed by both parties is recommended to confirm that all obligations have been met.

Finally, the chapter highlights closeout best practices: plan closure early, maintain accurate records throughout execution, communicate clearly with stakeholders, and address the human side of project endings—acknowledging that closeout can be an emotional time for team members.

Knowledge Nuggets

Chapter Pro Tip: Project managers are remembered for their delivery, so ensure financial success.

As stated at the start of this chapter, project managers are usually remembered by their project sponsors and clients for their project delivery and approach to closeout. Therefore, if financial success is critical to the client, ensure you deliver it.

Client needs and wants can take many forms. For example, we have worked on projects where financial considerations ranged from most to least important. So at the start of each project, ask, "What does success look like to you?" to determine the client's specific goals and importance.

Some specific financial goals might include:

- Meeting the budget (within a reasonable percentage, usually 5-10%)
- Achieving specified savings through the use of the project result
- Earning a set amount of revenue with the project result

No matter the goals, ensure they are factored into the planning, measured, and met upon project handover.

CHAPTER **16**

Chapter 16: Artificial Intelligence Tools

Generative AI is rapidly transforming the world, and project management is no exception to its wide-ranging benefits. Budgeting has relied heavily on historical data, manual estimation techniques, and project managers' experience until recently, but with the advent of generative AI, more accurate and adaptive forecasting and budget management are now possible.

PMI's Infinity, built on Microsoft CoPilot and trained on all PMI standards, would be a good choice for this transformative work. Infinity and other AI tools offer a powerful complement to project managers' techniques, regardless of the standards and methodologies used, enabling them to analyze vast datasets and spreadsheets, identify patterns, forecast outcomes, and make financial predictions as required.

The application of AI-based tools for financial management aligns with the overall principles of the PMBOK Guide and the Finance performance domain. By drawing parallels between AI-driven budgeting practices and the PMBOK Guide's structured focus areas, project managers can better understand how to integrate these tools while maintaining the rigor of their chosen methodology.

AI systems can provide valuable insights to support project managers' decision-making across all four Finance performance domain processes.

Enhancing Cost Planning

Cost planning includes selecting estimation techniques, defining units of measure, and establishing reporting formats.

AI tools can significantly strengthen this stage by:

- **Analyzing historical project frameworks** to recommend optimal cost management strategies
- **Identifying risk factors early**, based on patterns from similar projects
- **Customizing governance models** depending on project complexity and industry benchmarks

For example, machine learning algorithms can review thousands of past projects to suggest whether a parametric or analogous estimation approach is more suitable. This aligns with the PMBOK Guide's emphasis on tailoring processes to the project environment.

In essence, AI enables a more data-informed version of the thoughtful, context-aware planning the PMBOK Guide already recommends.

Transforming Cost Estimation

Cost estimation is one of the most challenging aspects of project management. AI enhances each of the major estimation techniques:

Augmented Expert Judgment: AI does not replace experts—it augments them. By providing data-driven insights, AI tools allow experts to validate their assumptions against empirical evidence.

Advanced Parametric Models: AI-driven parametric estimation can incorporate hundreds of variables simultaneously, far beyond what traditional spreadsheet models can handle. These systems can account for factors like market volatility, labor trends, geographic differences, and even weather patterns.

Automated Bottom-Up Estimation: AI tools can break down project scopes into granular components and assign cost estimates automatically, learning from previous work breakdown structures (WBS). This directly supports the bottom-up estimating method while dramatically reducing effort.

Predictive Three-Point Estimation: Instead of relying solely on optimistic, pessimistic, and most-likely estimates provided by humans, AI can generate probabilistic distributions based on historical patterns of uncertainty.

The result is a shift from static estimates to dynamic, continuously refined projections while still aligned with structured estimation techniques.

Bringing Accuracy to Budgets

Once individual costs are estimated, they are aggregated into a cost baseline, and contingency and management reserves are allocated.

AI tools bring several advantages here:

- **Real-time aggregation** of cost elements across complex portfolios

- **Scenario analysis**, allowing project managers to test multiple budget configurations instantly
- **Optimization algorithms** that suggest the most efficient allocation of resources

For example, AI can simulate different funding scenarios and recommend one that minimizes risk while maximizing value delivery. This directly supports guidance on balancing constraints and ensuring financial feasibility.

Additionally, AI can improve the accuracy of contingency reserves by analyzing historical variance and identifying realistic buffers, rather than relying on arbitrary percentages.

Reinventing Cost Control

Good project managers track, review, and regulate project costs, as well as manage changes to the cost baseline. AI enhances this process through:

Real-Time Monitoring: AI systems can continuously track expenditures against the budget, flagging deviations as they occur rather than after the fact.

Predictive Analytics: Instead of simply reporting that a project is over budget, AI can predict future overruns weeks or months in advance. This enables proactive decision-making.

Earned Value Management (EVM) Automation: EVM is a key technique for cost control in many large, complex projects. However, the difficulty in maintaining the data and calculating the formulas discourages its use. AI tools can automate EVM calculations and enhance them with predictive insights, such as more accurate forecasting of the Estimate at Completion (EAC).

Anomaly Detection: AI can identify unusual spending patterns that may indicate inefficiencies, errors, or even fraud. This adds a layer of governance that goes beyond traditional manual reviews and audits.

Continuous Learning: As the project progresses, AI systems refine their models based on actual performance, improving future forecasts and recommendations.

This transforms cost control from a reactive process into a proactive, intelligence-driven function while still adhering to a goal of maintaining financial discipline.

Risk Management Integration

Although Finance is a distinct performance domain in the PMBOK Guide, it is closely linked to the Risk Performance Domain. AI strengthens this integration by:

- Quantifying financial impacts of risks with greater precision
- Running Monte Carlo simulations at scale
- Identifying hidden correlations between risks and cost drivers

For example, AI might detect that supplier delays historically correlate with a 15% increase in labor costs, allowing project managers to adjust budgets proactively.

Benefits of AI-Driven Budgeting

Improved Accuracy: AI reduces reliance on assumptions by grounding estimates in historical and present data. When combined with human review of results, this improves budget accuracy.

Faster Decision-Making: Automated analysis enables quicker responses to change and more data-informed decisions.

Enhanced Transparency: Data-driven insights make it easier to justify budget decisions to stakeholders.

Scalability: AI tools can handle complex, multi-project environments with ease while following the rules of any project management governance and delivery model they have been trained on.

Continuous Improvement: Machine learning ensures that budgeting processes evolve.

Challenges and Considerations

Despite its advantages, integrating AI into project budgeting is not without challenges:

Data and Prompt Quality: AI is only as good as the data it processes. Poor-quality data can lead to misleading or incorrect outputs. Furthermore, the quality of the prompt the user gives to the AI tool will directly impact the output quality.

Applying Human Intelligence: All AI tools include disclaimers highlighting their limitations and emphasizing that their outputs may not always be accurate, complete, or reliable. These disclaimers remind users to exercise judgment before making decisions based on AI-generated content.

Integration with Existing Frameworks and Resources: Organizations must ensure that AI tools align with established methodologies such as the PMBOK Guide, rather than replacing frameworks or people. AI should not, and never should, operate without human validation, owing to accountability considerations.

Chapter Summary

The integration of AI into project budgeting represents a significant step forward in the evolution of project management. By enhancing accuracy, enabling predictive insights, and supporting real-time decision-making, AI tools address many of the limitations of traditional budgeting approaches.

At the same time, the principles of PMBOK remain as relevant as ever. Rather than replacing established methodologies, AI complements them, bringing new levels of efficiency and intelligence to well-defined processes.

For project managers, the challenge is not whether to adopt AI, but how to do so effectively. Those who succeed will be the ones who combine the discipline of a methodology or framework with the power of AI, creating a new standard for project cost management that is both structured and adaptive, rigorous and innovative.

In this convergence lies the future of project budgeting: a discipline grounded in proven frameworks, yet elevated by intelligent technology to meet the demands of an increasingly complex world.

References

China Briefing News. "China's Accounting Standards: Chinese GAAP vs. US GAAP and IFRS," May 31, 2017. https://www.china-briefing.com/news/china-gaap-vs-u-s-gaap-and-ifrs/.

Cohn, Michael. "Estimating with T-Shirt Sizes." Mike Cohn's Blog at Mountain Goat Software (blog). Mountain Goat Software, 2013. https://www.mountaingoatsoftware.com/blog/estimating-with-tee-shirt-sizes.

Council on Foreign Relations (CFR). "China's Massive Belt and Road Initiative," 2020. https://www.cfr.org/backgrounder/chinas-massive-belt-and-road-initiative.

Gartenberg, Chaim. "Apple Is Reportedly Going to Make More of Its Own Chips." The Verge, December 16, 2021. https://www.theverge.com/2021/12/16/22839850/apple-office-develop-chips-in-house-broadcom-skyworks.

Gallo, Amy. "A Refresher on Net Present Value." Harvard Business Review, November 19, 2014. https://hbr.org/2014/11/a-refresher-on-net-present-value.

Goodpasture, John C. *Quantitative Methods in Project Management*. Boca Raton FL: J. Ross Pub, 2004.

Greiman, V, and RDH Warburton. "Deconstructing the Big Dig: Best Practices for Mega-Project Cost Estimating." Orlando FL: PMI, 2009. https://www.pmi.org/learning/library/practices-mega-project-cost-estimating-6668.

Investopedia. "International Financial Reporting Standards (IFRS)." 2021. https://www.investopedia.com/terms/i/ifrs.asp.

Investopedia. "Understanding Cash: Definition, Types, and History." 2026. https://www.investopedia.com/terms/c/cash.asp#toc-what-is-cash.

Investopedia. "Understanding Counterpurchase: A Key Form of Countertrade." 2026. https://www.investopedia.com/terms/c/counterpurchase.asp.

IRS. "Virtual Currencies | Internal Revenue Service," March 11, 2022. https://www.irs.gov/businesses/small-businesses-self-employed/virtual-currencies.

Lehmann, Oliver F. *Project Business Management*. Best Practices and Advances in Program Management Series. Boca Raton FL: CRC Press, Taylor & Francis Group, 2019.

Lewis, James P. Project Planning, Scheduling & Control: The Ultimate Hands-on Guide to Bringing Projects in on Time and on Budget. 5th ed. New York NY: McGraw-Hill, 2011.

Meredith, Jack R., Scott M. Shafer, and Samuel J. Mantel. *Project Management in Practice*. Sixth edition. Hoboken NJ: Wiley, 2017.

Mill, Peter. "Utilising Rolling Wave Planning to Meet Funding Challenges." Association for Project Management, November 24, 2020. https://www.apm.org.uk/blog/utilising-rolling-wave-planning-to-meet-funding-challenges/.

Mitre. "Agile Cost Estimation." 2022. https://aida.mitre.org/agile/agile-cost-estimation/.

Morris, Rick A. *Stop Playing Games! A Project Manager's Guide to Successfully Navigating Organizational Politics*. Minnetonka MN: RMC Publications Inc, 2010.

Mountain Goat Software. “Planning Poker,” 2020. https://www.mountaingoatsoftware.com/agile/planning-poker.

Project Management Institute, ed. *A Guide to the Project Management Body of Knowledge* (PMBOK Guide). Sixth edition. Newtown Square PA: Project Management Institute, Inc, 2017.

---. *A Guide to the Project Management Body of Knowledge* (PMBOK Guide). Eighth edition. Newtown Square PA: Project Management Institute, Inc, 2025.

---. *Practice Standard for Earned Value Management*. Second edition. Newtown Square PA: Project Management Institute Inc. 2021.

---. *The PMI Project Management Fact Book*. 2nd ed. Newtown Square PA: Project Management Institute, 2001.

Pyle, William W., and Kermit D. Larson. *Fundamental Accounting Principles*. 9th ed. The Willard J. Graham Series in Accounting. Homewood, Ill. : Georgetown ONT: R.D. Irwin ; Irwin-Dorsey, 1981.

Venkataraman, Ray R., and Jeffrey K. Pinto. *Cost and Value Management in Projects*. Hoboken NJ: John Wiley & Sons, 2008.

Wikipedia. 2020. “Countertrade.” Last modified May 24. https://en.wikipedia.org/wiki/Countertrade.

---. 2021. “Program Evaluation and Review Technique.” Last modified November 5. https://en.wikipedia.org/w/index.php?title=Program_evaluation_and_review_technique&oldid=1053710479.

Appendix A: License to Use and Modify Templates and Instructional Materials

Book buyers are granted access to tools and templates, provided "as is" and may freely use and modify them to meet their needs. However, we always appreciate recognition of the templates' source. For those who need additional help, we offer training and consulting.

Please visit https://accidentalpm.online/downloads to access these materials. After registration, which takes 30 seconds or less, an account will be created, a link and password will be emailed to you, and the downloads will be accessible in your library. In addition, materials from our other publications (*Accidental Project Manager: Zero to Hero in 7 Days, Accidental Agile Project Manager: Zero to Hero in 7 Iterations, Risk Assessment Framework: Successfully Navigating Uncertainty*, and *Project Cost Management: Principles, Tools, Techniques, and Best Practices for Project Finance*) are accessible in the same online location.

If an email with account information is not found, sign in at https://accidentalpm.online/login, use the registration email address, and click the "Forgot Password" link.

Additional materials may be available for instructors who use this book for their classes. Please get in touch with us for further information. Need assistance with our site or have additional questions? Please get in touch with us at support@ppcgroup.us or by using the contact page at https://accidentalpm.online/contact.

Appendix B: Rules of Rounding

Rounding is a small but important part of producing accurate, defensible project estimates. While estimates are expected to include an accuracy estimate (PMI 2001), scientifically doing so is complicated unless multiple estimates are used, as in PERT. On the other hand, estimates are already guesses. Making an inaccurate guess on top of what may already be a guess would not provide the best estimates.

In most cases, project estimates can be made using whole numbers. Therefore, we only need to worry about fractional hours, or "cents," when paying bills and receiving payments.

Therefore, it is recommended to use appropriate rounding rules to provide slightly more generous, understandable estimates. Senior management needs to know the project will be about 3 years, not 3.32 years.

Four simple rules are:

1. One half or more rounds up, less than a half round down. Therefore, 4.499 rounds to 4 and 4.500 rounds to 5.

2. Do not use more precision than the least precise number. This follows the rule of significant figures: when adding or subtracting numbers, the result cannot be more precise than the least precise input. For example, when adding x.xx and y.y, the answer should be rounded to z.z.

3. Two decimal digits are appropriate when dealing with fractions representing percentages, as they will be whole numbers as percentages. For example, 0.86 is 86%.

4. When dealing with a series of computations, round at every step to avoid false precision. For highly sensitive calculations, keep internal precision and round only the final result. For project estimates, rounding at each step is usually more straightforward and more practical. For example,

   Step 1: 7.333 x 2 = 14.666 rounds to 15.
   Step 2: 15 / 3 = 5.

If Excel or similar tools are used for calculations, be careful. When formatting a cell to round, precision can be lost, especially when dealing with many decimal numbers of varying lengths. Precision is lost because only the display is changed. For example, Display formatting 4.567 to two decimal places displays as 4.57, but it still calculates as 4.567. Subsequent computations will use the unrounded value. Using the ROUND() function in Excel to round numbers is more accurate. The function rounds the actual value, not just the displayed value.

Excel also provides ROUNDUP() and ROUNDDOWN(), which always round in one direction. These should be used only when applying conservative or aggressive rounding rules intentionally.
Suppose a calculator is used instead of Excel. In that case, most calculators have a feature that performs calculations with whole

numbers or a fixed number of decimal places. Use these settings for good rounding. For example, with a 1-decimal setting, 12.46 displays and calculates as 12.5, and 12.44 displays and calculates as 12.4.

Appendix C: More About PERT

To start, let us look at a complete example. Suppose we have a project with three tasks (A, B, and C). Further, the pessimistic (P), optimistic (O), and most likely (M) estimates for the task durations are known. Finally, only human resources work on these tasks, and their rates are known. Therefore, we can convert the schedule estimates to cost estimates.

The cost estimates have been provided (units do not matter as long as they are consistent; if it helps, consider these in the thousands of dollars). Our goal is to estimate the total cost to complete the project with 2-sigma (approximately 95%) confidence. The formulas are in the first and last rows.

TASK	P ($000)	M ($000)	O ($000)	PERT Estimate ($000)	VARIANCE
A	45	27	14	(P+O+4M)/6	$((P-O)/6)^2$
B	90	60	40		
C	45	44	39		
Total				$\sum(A+B+C)$	$\sqrt{\sum A+B+C}$

Figure 10: PERT Example

We can now complete the chart using the standard rounding rules (Appendix B).

TASK	P ($000)	M ($000)	O ($000)	PERT Estimate ($000)	VARIANCE
A	45	27	14	167/6=28	5^2=25
B	90	60	40	370/6=62	64
C	45	44	39	260/6=43	1
Total				A + B + C = 133	$\sqrt{25+64+1}$ =9

Figure 11: Completed PERT Example

The PERT estimate for the project is $133,000 +/- $18,000 with about 95% confidence. While it is possible to continue doubling to increase confidence in the estimate, going beyond 95% typically makes the range unrealistic. It will eventually encompass the entire budget (e.g., $133,000 +/- $133,000).

Now that the estimate is known, PERT has additional power. We can answer "what if" questions about the estimate using standard mathematics. These may be questions such as

- How confident are we if our budget was only $110,000?
- If we want to be 75% confident, what should our budget be?

We can answer these questions if

- the tasks are serial (one must be completed before the next begins)
- we assume each task is relatively independent.

If these conditions are accurate, we can assume that a normal curve distribution is possible.

Suppose we assume a 50:50 chance of completing the project at the estimated cost of $133,000. In that case, we can use a normal distribution curve to compute other possibilities. Fortunately, Excel has a function that performs the calculations for us.

If we want to find the confidence of a $110,000 budget, if D is the desired budget (110), M is our PERT computed budget (133), and SQRT(σ^2_μ) is the calculated range (18):

NORMDIST(D, M, SQRT(σ^2_μ), TRUE)

Equation 18: Excel Normal Distribution Function

Making the substitution and considering other possibilities indicates that, if our budget is cut to $110,000, there is only 10% confidence we can complete the budget with that amount.

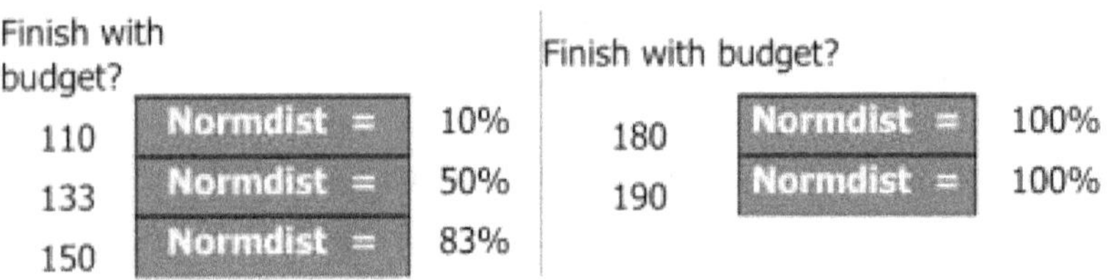

Figure 12: Applying the Normal Distribution Curve to Potential Budgets

Our example is a small project; however, the same principles apply to larger projects. For example, suppose we compute the probability for each task's cost estimate individually. In that case, we can multiply them together to determine the likelihood for the entire project.

Now consider the second question: given the desired confidence level, what should our budget be? Again, we can use the Excel NORMINV function to compute the required funding for any specified probability of success.

$$\text{NORMINV (Probability, M, SQRT}(\sigma^2_\mu))$$

Equation 19: Excel NORMINV Function

Substituting the values and considering other possibilities, if the client wants 95% confidence, we can complete the project for $163,000. On the other hand, if 75% is "good enough," we could estimate the budget as $145,000.

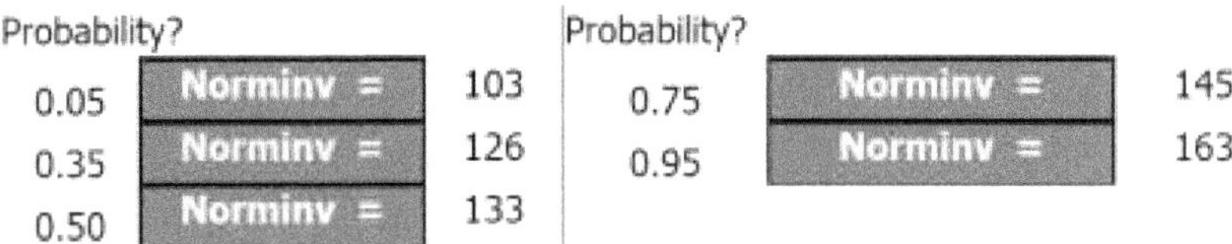

Figure 13: Applying the Normal Distribution Curve Inverse Function to Potential Probabilities

In conclusion, we have a mathematical means of improving the chances of success in virtually any situation involving units of measurement (e.g., time, dollars) and the probabilities of reaching them. In recognition that we cannot demand risk-free projects, for example, $150,000 with an 83% probability of success might be reasonable. On the other hand, if stakeholders strongly desire to meet the $170,000 budget, then 98% probability might be appropriate. We know what we can negotiate and have data to provide stakeholders to inform decision-making using these techniques.

INDEX

A

Acceptance, 13
acceptance test cases, 13
as contract element, 153
confirming project outcomes, 175
contract clauses and cost impact, 155
Operational acceptance, 175
risk allocation in contracts, 162
stakeholder satisfaction milestone, 178
testing and quality assurance, 171
acquisition, 49, 104
Actual cost (AC), 143, 149
Agreement, 74, 154, 162
AI systems, 182
allocation of risk, 162
amortization, 86, 88
Arbitration, 154–155
architectural work, 130

B

BAC (Budget at Completion), 146–148
balance sheet, 86–87
Baselining, 34, 55
Basis of Estimate (BoE), 57, 76, 78
beta distributions, 46–48, 65
BOO (Build, Own, Operate), 105
Breach, 155
Budget policies, 60
budget variance, 31–33, 129
Budget performance, 56
budgeting best practices, 101
budgets, 12–14, 16, 24, 28, 30, 33, 41, 56, 85, 89, 92, 97–99, 126, 131–132, 165, 168–169, 172, 178, 183, 185
operations budgets, 13
Build, Lease, and Transfer (BLT), 106, 113
Build, Operate, and Transfer (BOT), 106, 113
business case, 38–39, 50
buyback, 110, 113

C

Capital Budgeting, 86–87, 92–93
overview and stakeholder planning, 57
capital expenses, 104
cash flow, 82, 109, 113, 165–167
Cash Flow Forecast, 166, 168
cash inflow, 166, 168
cash on delivery, 119
cash outflow, 166, 168

Estimated cash flow, 127
feasibility studies, role, 127
in-house vs. outsourced cost decisions, 128
negative cash flow, 168
change control, 12
change procedures, 162
change requests, 13, 152
cost change control, 56
closure plan, 175
Communication, 177
completion date, 126, 163
Cone of Uncertainty, 72, 78
consensus, 102
contract types, 156, 158, 162
contractors, 117, 163, 166
contracts, 38, 157
closeout best practices, 176, 178
closure and financial reconciliation, 173–174
incentive clauses and stakeholder alignment, 163
legal framework overview, 153
payment methods and structures, 121
resource procurement and planning, 7
scope and cost implications of wording, 117
standard and special clauses, 155
types: fixed-price, T&M, cost-reimbursement, incentive, 156
control charts, 129
conventional financing, 107–108, 113
cost accountant, 31, 33, 94, 103
work location, 55
cost baseline, 9, 11, 82
See also Unknown
definition and approval, 81
project financing and stakeholder approval, 10
vs. contingency reserves, 92
cost categorization, 92
cost control, 2, 127, 184
See also monitoring and control; cost management
AI and advanced analytics, 185
contract types and incentives, 158
contractual and legal frameworks, 153, 162
cost control methods, 60
cost overrun, 32
earned value management, 149
overview and importance, 3
performance measurement and variance analysis, 56

policies, procedures, and formats, 60
project finance and stakeholder considerations, 104
trend analysis and variance detection tools, 125, 135
work authorization systems, 159
cost management, 3, 27, 188
See also project management; cost control
as knowledge area overview, 33
cost baseline creation and updating, 54
Cost Management Approach, 54
Cost Management Plan development, 8, 82
financing methods (loans, equity, BOO, BOT), 20
processes: planning, estimating, budgeting, controlling, 7
project success, impact, 11, 28
cost of capital, 112, 114
cost of borrowing, 20
Cost performance index (CPI), 144–150
cost variance, 129, 149–150
cost-benefit analysis, 39
cryptocurrency payments, 121
currency, 88–89, 119–121
budgeting and documentation conventions, 55
currency conversions, 88, 92–93
unit of measure in earned value management, 140

D

debt, 113, 115–116, 169
as cost of capital, 112
debt financing, 111, 113
project financing structures, 107, 109
types and definitions, 108
Determine Budget, 9, 16
Direct costs, 83–84, 93
discount rate, 22, 45
discounting, 21, 24
dividends, 20, 24, 111, 114, 122
documentation, 55, 177
archiving and lessons learned, 174
cost estimates and planning, 13
current records for closeout, 176
financial management plan template, 54
knowledge capture and handoffs, 137
duration, 78

E

EAC (Estimate at Completion), 146–147, 185
Earned Value Management, 139–141, 149, 151, 184
earned value (EV), 141–144, 149, 160, 162
Earned Value methods, 56
earned value rules, 59
effort, 74, 78, 142, 145, 149, 183
equity, 20, 107–108, 112
equity financing, 111
equity investors, 113
Estimated Monetary Value (EMV), 70, 92
estimates, 2, 73–74, 95, 101
AI and automation, 183, 186
Analogous estimates, 63
basis of estimate (BoE), 76–77
budget formation, role, 10–11, 98, 168
confidence ranges, 78
contingency and reserves, 70, 83
contracting and procurement, 29, 120
documentation and assumptions, 48, 56, 59, 97
Estimation techniques, 60
iterative review and timing, 102
parametric estimates, 63, 183
techniques and methods, 8, 16, 63–65, 78
three-point estimates, 63–64, 78
uncertainty and confidence ranges, 33, 61
Estimation Accuracy, 68, 78
ETC (Estimate to Complete), 146, 149–150
Eurotunnel, 107–108, 113
execution, 11, 13, 135, 162
closeout activities, 178
cost control during, 126
cost estimating and budgeting, 69
execution controls, 126
financial reviews and oversight, 132
predictable execution, 162
records and financial data maintenance, 176
work authorization systems, formality, 161

F

fast-tracking, 126
Feasibility, 127–128, 135, 184
Fibonacci numbers, 74
finance professionals, 27
financial analysis, 39, 50
Financial Closure, 173–176
financial activities, 174
financial performance domain, 1, 7, 11, 13, 17, 53, 181–182
financial planning, 86, 120

financial regulations, 133–135
financial statements, 87, 175
Fixed costs, 84
flexibility, 27, 93
Force Majeure, 155
frameworks, 187–188
Function Point Analysis (FPA), 67–68, 78–79
Future Value, 21–22, 24

G

general contractor, 165
governance, 54
AI-driven oversight and anomaly detection, 185–186
budgeting constraints and scope adjustments, 33
governance roles, 59
work authorization systems and approval processes, 160–162

H

health and safety, 13

I

IFRS (International Financial Reporting Standards), 134
incentive clause, 163
incentive payments, 121
incremental approach, 91–92
indirect costs, 83–84, 93
inflation, 23–24, 29, 72, 93
Intangible costs, 84
Integration, 172, 185, 188
financial domain interaction points, 57
frameworks and methodologies alignment, 187
intellectual property, 155
interest, 20, 24, 49, 104–105, 107, 111, 115, 119, 122, 151, 166
basic concept defined, 19
compound interest, 19, 21
cost of financing, 114
debt types and pricing, 108
discounting future cash flows, 22
interest rate, 22
Simple interest, 19
time value of money, 21
Internal Rate of Return (IRR), 45, 50
invoices, 88–89, 118–122, 133, 151–152, 154, 168, 174, 178

J

J-curve, 130–131

L

Lessons learned, 71, 133, 176
loan funds, 165
loans, 57, 88, 104–105, 107, 111, 113, 115
as senior debt, repayment priority, 108
unsecured loans, 104

M

mezzanine debt, 108
milestones, 39, 76, 118, 141–142, 149
Monitor and Control Finances, 8, 16
monitoring and control, 11–12
  See also cost control
Monte Carlo simulation, 78, 185

N

net cash, 167–168
NPV (net present value), 44, 50

O

oil and gas exploration, 46
operational activities, 175

P

payback period, 50
percent complete, 141
  Physical Percent Complete, 141
performance measurement, 160, 162
performance measures, 42, 50, 56, 149
PERT (Program Evaluation and Review Technique), 9, 64–66, 69, 78–79
Plan Cost Management, 8, 16, 53–54, 59–60, 76, 132
planned expenditures, 160
planned value (PV), 142–144, 149
Planning Fallacy, 72, 78
Planning Poker, 73–74
PMBOK® Guide (Project Management Body of Knowledge Guide), 1, 7, 31, 81–83, 181–183, 187–188
  PMBOK Performance Domain, 15
portfolio, 46
  business case and cost-benefit analysis, 38, 51
  early financing and financial planning, 48
  financial metrics and valuation (NPV), 44
  portfolio management system, 37, 50
  portfolio risk, 50
  risk vs. individual project risk, 47
  strategic project selection and alignment, 37, 50
predictive analytics, 184
predictive methods, 2–3
  See also predictive projects
present value, 21–22, 24, 44
procurement, 7, 14, 16–17, 31, 33, 57, 59, 125, 158, 165
  procurement requirements, 59
  procurement specialists, 14
profit and loss (P&L) statement, 87–88
program management, 30, 91
project charter, 8–9, 29, 37–38
project closeout, 13, 176–178
  project records, 176

Project Termination, 172
project finance, 57, 88, 93, 103–105, 107, 113
project initiation, 12, 48
project lifecycle, 3, 16, 23
project management, 2–3, 16, 23, 132, 188
See also cost management
Cost planning, 182
definition and scope, 1
predictive projects, 91
project budget, 81, 101
project management knowledge areas, 11
Project Management Office (PMO), 17, 27, 103
project management plan, 8, 53
project management practices, 132
work authorization and governance, 160
project managers
budget responsibilities, varying levels, 27–28
collaboration with financial experts, 31, 113
cost estimation role, 23, 97, 101
financial planning and budgeting, 3, 10, 33, 59, 70, 102
monitoring and controlling costs, 13, 87, 149, 184, 188
project closeout activities, 172, 176
project financing structures, 81, 134, 155, 162
project plan, 69, 126
See also project management plan
Project planning, 61, 68, 176
project risk, 46–48, 50
project schedule, 2, 12–14, 30, 33, 65, 69, 76, 91, 118, 136, 143, 148–149, 151, 160–161, 163, 174, 176
project selection, 3, 19, 37, 50
project selection criteria, 37
project selection tools, 50
project sponsor, 125–126
Project Structures, 105
Project team members, 70
public-private partnerships (PPPs), 105

R

reimbursable-cost contracts, 117
reporting, 132, 134, 178
AI tools and predictive analytics, 182
budget storage and version control, 55
cost monitoring and control, 9, 56
earned value management data, 142

expenditure and invoice tracking, 151–152
reserves, 13, 17, 59, 93, 97
AI tools in estimation, 183–184
computation and allocation, 83, 89–90
contingency reserves, 9, 12–13, 30, 34, 70, 82–83, 90, 92, 97–99
contingency vs. management reserves, 70, 82, 92
in planning and budgeting, 9, 16, 55
management reserves, 9, 70, 81–82, 90, 92
resource availability, 160, 162
resources, 12, 57, 126, 136, 172–173, 175
allocation and planning, 13, 37, 67
availability and work authorization, 160, 162
cost estimation and budgeting, 29, 31, 93
influence on scope and schedule, 16, 130
leveling and smoothing, 76
optimization via AI and algorithms, 187
procurement and contract management, 156, 165
risk management impacts, 70
tangible vs. intangible categories, 83–84
Return, 42–43, 47
expected return, 47
Internal Rate of (IRR), 45
ROACE (Return on Average Capital Employed), 50
ROI (return on investment), 43–44, 50
time value of money and reinvestment, 19–20
revenue, 46, 48, 81–82, 85, 94, 106, 115, 167, 169, 179
BOO and BOT project financing, 104–105, 113
payback period calculations, 45
risk management, 14, 30, 163, 185
risk analysis, 89
Risk Management Plan, 58
risk management process, 83
ROA (return on assets), 42, 50
roles and responsibilities, 54
rolling wave planning, 91–92
root cause analysis, 129
rules, 29, 56, 61–62, 96, 122
budget decision-making and justification, 186
cost control and baseline management, 59
financial reporting standards, IFRS, 134
reserves, contingency and management, 70

S

S-curve, 130–131
scenario analysis, 184
schedule baseline, 160, 162
schedule performance index (SPI), 144–145, 149–150
Schedule Variance (SV), 149–150
scope, 139
budgeting and estimation accuracy, 16, 30, 67, 72
changes and re-planning, 126
constraints: time, resources, risk, 70
contractual and governance controls, 37, 117, 160, 162
stakeholder and financial collaboration, 33
scoring models, 40
senior debt, 108
sign-off, 176
stakeholders, 16, 33, 151
buy-in for cost estimates, 38, 70, 74
communication and reporting needs, 13, 93, 97, 132
cost management plan approval, 56
external economic factors, influence, 72
funding decisions, influence, 104
project closure involvement, 177–178
re-baselining and re-planning, 34, 102
transparency in financial reporting, 186
standard deviations, 78
statement of work, 156
story points, 73–75, 78
systemic risk, 46

T

taxation, 14, 29, 72, 83, 85–86, 92–93, 96, 101
tax concessions, 105
TCPI (To Complete Performance Index), 147–150
terms and conditions, 162
time value of money, 19, 24–25, 45, 122
time-and-materials contracts, 162
transparency, 48, 78

U

useful life, 86–87

V

VAC (variance at completion), 146–147, 150
variances, 78, 125, 143–144, 149, 151, 174
Variance thresholds, 59

W

WBS Dictionary, 95
weighted averages, 78
work authorization, 160–162
work authorization system, 159
work order, 160
work package release, 160
Work Breakdown Structure (WBS), 8–9, 13, 16, 62–63, 66–67, 72, 76, 95, 97–98, 101, 118, 121, 183

MORE PPC GROUP, LLC PUBLICATIONS

Accidental Project Manager (Amazon Bestseller #1)

The perfect companion to the *Accidental Agile Project Manager*! Learn more about managing predictive or waterfall projects.

Each chapter includes a project management tip, reading selections from the PMBOK® Guide, and additional learning resources. In addition, more than a dozen ready-to-use templates are available online.

Available in all Amazon marketplaces.
Paperback ASIN: 171879293X
Kindle ASIN: B07F714CMN
Audiobook ASIN: B093LKMTXR

Risk Assessment Framework (Amazon Bestseller #2)

Ready for more project management knowledge? *The Risk Assessment Framework provides a comprehensive framework and implementation recommendations to establish a reusable,* sustainable risk management methodology for any initiative. In addition, tools, templates, forms, and guidance support the framework's performance.

Whether you are an aspiring, new, accidental, or experienced manager, this book will help you successfully navigate uncertainty for any initiative.

Available in all Amazon marketplaces.
Paperback ASIN: 0989377075

Kindle ASIN: B07ZML9GW5

Accidental Agile Project Manager (Amazon Bestseller #3)

The perfect companion to the *Accidental Project Manager*! Learn more about managing agile projects.

Each chapter includes a project management tip, reading selections from the PMBOK® Guide, and additional learning resources. In addition, more than a dozen ready-to-use templates are available online.

Available in all Amazon marketplaces.
Paperback ASIN: 0989377091
Kindle ASIN: B08L168NTJ
Audiobook ASIN: B09LYNV72D

GET YOUR FREE TEMPLATES!

As a valued reader, you have access to all the templates referenced in this book and those accompanying our other books!

Sign up for access (you keep the downloads, plus they are in your online library) at:

accidentalpm.online/downloads

Bonus: Our PM Best Practices and Tips will be delivered to your inbox monthly.

www.ingramcontent.com/pod-product-compliance
Lightning Source LLC
LaVergne TN
LVHW050624100826
845148LV00011B/1726

* 9 7 8 1 7 3 5 6 2 1 3 3 3 *